D1270095

The Go-Go

CHICAGO WHITE SOX

The Go-Go

CHICAGO WHITE SOX

by Dave Condon

FOREWORD BY BILL VEECK

The Coward-McCann Sports Library

COWARD-McCANN, Inc.   New York

This book is for Don Maxwell, Wilfrid Smith, and Stewart Owen of the *Chicago Tribune*, Taylor Spink and Joseph E. Merrion, who were in Dave Condon's corner before he ever had a corner . . . and for the late Mrs. Grace Comiskey, who was and always will be baseball's first lady.

Foreword

by BILL VEECK

I feel privileged to have had a preview of *The Go-Go Chicago White Sox* as it rolled from the typewriter of my good friend David Condon. Some of the early history I knew, like Dave, from reading and listening to the old-timers who were close to the scene even before the turn of the century. The modern White Sox I knew more intimately, and during my association with other clubs, both in Chicago and in other American League cities, I was always aware of the White Sox and their heritage. I have seen Dave gathering his information on the modern White Sox by firsthand daily coverage in spring training and during the regular season. He has virtually lived with the men who were and are the "Go-Go Chicago White Sox."

As Dave reveals on the following pages, the saga of the White Sox was one of struggle, ingenuity, perseverance and finally success. After the White Sox were conceived by the "Old Roman," it was his personal conquest of the City of Chicago that gave the team life. Then came the lean years that followed the 1919 scandal of the "Black Sox," a series of circumstances that actually broke the heart of the Old Roman.

It took the unflinching determination on the part of the Comiskey family and their long-time friend and employee, the late Harry Grabiner — also a great friend and partner of mine in Cleveland — to keep the White Sox an integral part of the city of Chicago.

During the latter part of this campaign, waged so success-fully by the late Grace R. Comiskey, I was busily occupied with another Chicago ball club, but never lost sight of the hold the White Sox had on the public of Chicago. Be it tradi-tion or inborn stubbornness, the White Sox fan has a fierce loyalty the like of which I have never experienced in my years with the Chicago Cubs, Milwaukee Brewers, Cleveland Indians and the late, lamented St. Louis Browns. This, I might mention, was one important factor in our determination to purchase Mrs. Rigney's shares when they became available.

In the past, if you were born on the South Side of Chicago, you were a Sox fan from the time you saw the light of day. This is still true, but, through the efforts of a number of modern baseball figures, the White Sox have become even more of a city-wide, even nationwide, institution.

The advent of Frank Lane . . . Paul Richards . . . Al Lopez were milestones in the rebirth of the Chicago White Sox. The farm system, developed under the direction of Charles Comis-key and John Rigney, was also instrumental in the rise of the White Sox fortunes. It was a combination of all these, and as-tute trades and the contributions of farm hands, that enabled the Sox to climb to the American League pennant in 1959. The finest, most loyal baseball fans in the world — the Chicago White Sox fans — deserved that pennant and helped to win it. We hope to give them many more.

Contents

The Go-Go
CHICAGO WHITE SOX

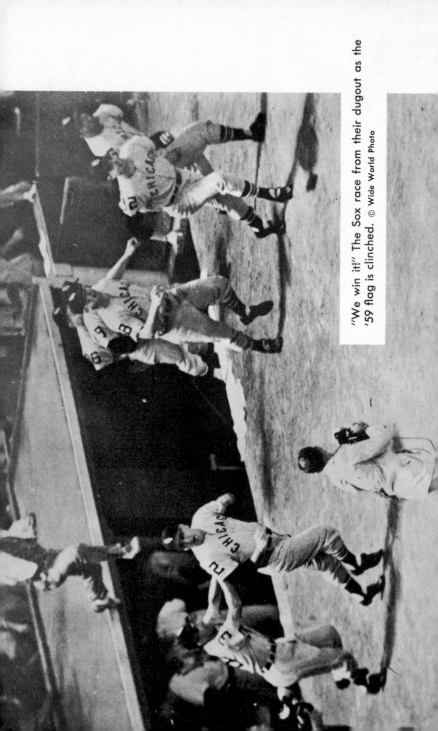

"We win it!" The Sox race from their dugout as the '59 flag is clinched. © Wide World Photo

CHAPTER 1

"The Magic Number Is None!"

FOR THIRTY-NINE years there had been only tears. Now champagne was flowing. The Chicago White Sox were champions of the American League, champions for the first time since that lamented autumn of 1919. The pennant drought of four decades had come to a spectacular end in Cleveland's mammoth Municipal Stadium only a few short hours earlier, when Luis Aparicio had touched off a game-ending double play to slam the door on Cleveland's pursuing Indians. The Go-Go White Sox had taken the 4–2 clincher on the home run hitting of Jim (Jungle) Rivera and Al Smith, and behind the stout pitching of Early Wynn, Bob Shaw, and Gerry Staley. So now, after thirty-nine years of tears, the champagne corks were popping against the drone of the giant United Air Lines charter speeding Chicago's heroes from Cleveland to Midway airport, where thousands of fans were whooping it up in these wee morning hours of September 23, 1959.

This was a happy band of heroes winging homeward with their championship. There was Pitcher Billy Pierce, the lethal little lefty who had worn White Sox flannels since 1949, slapping the broad back of first baseman Ted Kluszewski, the home run slugger who had just joined the club during the stretch drive. Second baseman Nellie Fox and some of his other nondrinking teammates kept the champagne flowing for the newspapermen, broadcasters, and club officials. Catcher Sherman Lollar sat shaking his head in disbelief. It seemed too good to be true.

As the airliner knifed through the night, sportscaster Jack Brickhouse, who with Lou Boudreau had telecast the game over WGN-TV, paced the aisles lining up interviews. By special arrangements with United, Brickhouse had arranged a broadcast direct from the plane. It was to begin the instant the plane winged over South Bend, Indiana.

Brickhouse paused alongside Nellie Fox, Luis Aparicio, and Early Wynn, who were to run in exactly that order in balloting for the American League's most valuable player of 1959. He asked, "Nellie, tell me something I've always wondered about. Do you remember ever swallowing your chewing tobacco?"

"Remember it!" Fox said. "I don't even want to think about it. But it happened once in Kansas City. I thought I'd swallowed a volcano."

Moving on, Brickhouse came to Pitcher Dick Donovan, a right-hander who had hit his major league stride with the White Sox after floundering in the Braves' organization. A king-sized cigar jutted from a corner of the big Irishman's face.

"And who do you think will pitch the World Series opener?" asked Brickhouse.

Tricky Dick shifted the cigar to the opposite corner of his mouth and said, "They're nuts if they don't pitch me.

"Say, what a thrill that'd be. The first White Sox World Series game since 1919. Bands playing. Flags flying. Fifty thousand fans jamming Comiskey Park. And out there on the mound, Dick Donovan — waiting for Staley to get in from the bull pen."

"You only say it because it's true," quipped Rivera. "And hey, whatever happened to the Yankees?"

It was a happy group of champions. And up front, in the compartment directly behind the cockpit, was the happiest of them all. That was Al Lopez, the handsome Hidalgo who in three seasons as White Sox skipper had led them to two second-place finishes and, finally, this championship.

Lopez lounged back and said, "This has been my most fantastic season in thirty-six years in baseball. These fellows never gave up. I said three years ago — when I came to Chicago — that the White Sox could win the pennant. I said the same thing last year, and we'd have won it, too, if we hadn't gotten off to such a horrible start.

"I'll never forget that miserable start. We were in eighth place in mid-May when we began a series with the Yanks. The Yanks looked like they were going to run away with it, with only five losses in twenty-four games, but we conceded nothing. We never gave up, and if you check, you'll find that from June 13 until the end of the 1958 season, we played .588 ball while the Yanks were playing .548 ball.

"That's why I was more confident than ever this spring — even when lots of the experts predicted we wouldn't save second place. We played good ball and we had the good luck every championship team needs. We were fortunate that Bob Shaw developed into a great starting pitcher and that Turk Lown and Gerry Staley gave us the best bull pen in the league. Early Wynn's twenty-two wins —at the age of thirty-nine — were sensational. A few years ago I said if there was one game I absolutely had to win, Early would be my pitcher. So you know who's going to open for the Sox in the World Series!"

Now Midway airport alerted the United pilots that the crowd of fans was swelling with each minute. Jack Brickhouse started his broadcast and had pitcher Bob Shaw at the mike. Charles A. (Chuck) Comiskey, grandson and namesake of the founder of the Chicago White Sox, was moving through the back of the plane congratulating the players. He tried to talk Ted Kluszewski out of the ball that had made the final put-out of the Cleveland games.

"Never," said Big Klu, a National Leaguer until White Sox President Bill Veeck had sprung him from the Pirates in mid-August. "I've been waiting fourteen years to get into a World Series. I'm going to have this baseball gold-plated."

"Good," said Comiskey. "Only remember, we got you to hit us some home runs. Hit us a couple in the Series."

"I'll hit at least a couple myself," broke in Dick Donovan.

"Whatever happened to the Yankees?" shouted Jim Rivera.

Thousands cheered as the airliner rolled to a stop on the

Jim Landis and Billy Pierce discuss a technical point.

National Guard aprons at Midway airport shortly after 2
A.M. Police details headed by Supervising Captain Joseph
Graney and Captain John L. Sullivan held back the fans until
prop blades stopped spinning.

Then the airliner door swung open and out came Bubba
Phillips, Jim Landis, Earl Torgeson, Sammy Esposito, Wynn,
Fox, Aparicio, Brickhouse, Comiskey, and such passionate
followers as Joe Meegan, Frank Darling, and Andy Frain, the
usher chief, who had accompanied the White Sox for that
one-night stand in Cleveland.

A band was playing the old song about Chicago being that
wonderful town; about State Street being that great street.
There were joyous howls. Pennants waved. And by the
hundreds they surged toward the plane, this dedicated breed
of Chicago South Siders whose loyalty and partisanship have
been matched in baseball only by those rabid Brooklynites
who lived and died with their beloved Bums in days long
gone by.

There were, among this wild welcoming audience, Howard
E. Wolfson and Jay Goldstein, box seat regulars at White
Sox Park since Cracker Schalk's tenure as manager. There
were Red McNamara, Jack Rafferty, Ad Elliott, and hundreds of their pals who had squirmed with them in the bleach-
ers during the trying years when the White Sox were regular
second-division tenants.

Mayor Richard J. Daley, whose bungalow home on Lowe
Avenue is only a pop fly from Comiskey Park, was up the
landing ramp steps the instant the first of the White Sox
appeared. With his family, the No. 1 White Sox fan had
watched the clinching game on television; then he had sped to
Midway, his enthusiasm dampened only by the misguided use
of Chicago's air raid sirens, which sent thousands of citizens
scurrying for refuge. But here, at this wonderful moment,
Mayor Daley stood smiling and laughing and pumping the
hands of the athletes who so often had chased foul balls to
his third-base box in Comiskey Park.

Whooping it up beside the mayor was a towheaded man, part fan, part executive, and part genius. He was Bill Veeck, who had purchased 54 per cent of the club early in 1959. With his pretty wife, Mary Frances, planting kisses here and there, Veeck slapped each back and clutched each hand as his White Sox descended the steps. His white sport shirt still was soaked with perspiration; literally and figuratively he had sweated out the final result of the game he most had wanted to see, and could not.

Veeck had been unable to make the Cleveland trip because a prior commitment — to make a speech, No. 362 of the year — kept him in Bloomington, down in central Illinois. During that speech, Veeck followed the White Sox progress through signals from a front-row guest who had a transistor radio. Afterward, he followed the last few innings on radio as Dizzy Trout sped him back to Chicago in the Go-Go Sox station wagon. He confessed that Trout had steered off the highway in that hectic minute when relief pitcher Gerry Staley was serving up his first and only pitch — an outside sinker that Cleveland's Vic Power hit into the concluding double play.

Trout had driven directly to Midway, where Bill was cheered by thousands, some of whom had known him since he was a smart-alecky kid tending the concessions for the Chicago Cubs, hated North Side rivals of the Sox.

Now, in happy confusion, the White Sox fought through the crowd to waiting taxicabs. Jim Rivera's cigar was snatched away. A radio announcer put five questions to promotion director Ed Short in the belief that he was Manager Lopez.

Again Rivera shouted, "Whatever happened to the Yankees?"

Bill Veeck said, "The magic number is none!"

Slowly the crowd of almost 50,000 melted away. Hours later they turned to their favorite baseball writers — Edward Prell and Robert Cromie of the *Chicago Tribune*, Warren

Brown and Wendell Smith of Chicago's *American*, John P. Carmichael and Howard Roberts of the *Chicago Daily News*, and Jerry Holtzman and Edgar Munzel of the Chicago *Sun-Times* — to relive the most thrilling single White Sox victory in forty years.

A Cleveland crowd of 54,293 had jammed double-decked Municipal Stadium to see if their gasping Indians, three and one-half games behind, could head off the White Sox.

Manager Al Lopez nominated Early Wynn, the antique right-hander who had won fourteen games in '58. This night, Wynn was bidding for his twenty-first victory of the year — his highest total since 1954, when he had captured twenty-three games for the pennant-winning Indians.

Cleveland manager Joe Gordon countered with Jim Perry, a twenty-two-year-old rookie right-hander who had been in the cradle when Wynn was an apprentice in the minor leagues.

In the second inning, Cleveland's Minnie Minoso — a refugee from the original White Sox Go-Go cast — attempted to speed home from third base on Rocky Colavito's fly ball to Al Smith. Smith threw on the run to John (Honey) Romano, the young catcher subbing for the ailing Lollar. Romano tagged out Minoso.

The White Sox stepped in front in the third. With one out, Bubba Phillips dropped a single in center. Wynn popped up to Woody Held but little Luis Aparicio cracked a double to the right field wall. Phillips streaked in with run number one as Colavito threw to Held, who was late on the relay to Russ Nixon. Nellie Fox walked. Then Billy Goodman doubled down the right field line, bringing in Aparicio. The White Sox led, 2–0.

But Cleveland, which had rallied magnificently after blowing a four-game series to the White Sox less than a month earlier, was not giving in so easily. Woody Held worked Wynn for a walk starting the Cleveland fifth. Wynn retaliated by striking out pinch batter Chuck Tanner. Rookie

"High as we'll go," says Skipper Lopez to Bill Veeck. He wasn't wrong in '59.

Gordon Coleman beat out a hit back of second. Jimmy Piersall singled to deep left center, scoring Held, but then Vic Power grounded into a double play.

Mudcat Grant was pitching for Cleveland when the White Sox came up in the sixth. Honey Romano's drive backed Piersall to the center field boundary. This signaled trouble for Grant, and it came quickly. Al Smith smashed a home run over the left field wire boundary. Jungle Jim Rivera followed with a homer to right. Now the White Sox had a four-to-one edge and could hear the pennant flapping.

Tito Francona got one of those runs back in an Indian uprising in the sixth. Wynn was replaced by Bob Shaw, the handsome twenty-six-year-old right-hander whose unexpected success spurred the White Sox during the hectic pennant year. With Shaw's appearance, Sherman Lollar came in to catch despite a bruised right hand. Manager Lopez was pulling out the stops.

In the ninth, Shaw got Held to pop up. But then Jim Baxes slashed a single off Shaw's glove. Relief pitcher Jack Harshman followed with a single to right, putting Ray Webster (who was running for Baxes) on third. Webster stayed on third when Piersall's single caromed off Fox's glove. Now the bases were filled with Indians and Al Lopez trudged from the dugout.

At the mound, the grim-faced Chicago manager patted Shaw and awaited the appearance of thirty-nine-year-old Gerry Staley, bellwether of the relief corps. Upstairs, Cleveland manager Frank Lane moaned: "There should be a law against using that Staley more than five times a week."

This indeed was Staley's sixty-fifth appearance, and it was to be his most memorable. His first pitch was an outside sinker. Power took a swing. Aparicio glided to his left, speared the ball, sprinted four steps, kicked second base to force Piersall, and then rifled to Big Klu at first base to double Power and end the game.

For thirty-nine years there had been only tears. Now it was time for champagne. The White Sox stormed from the dugout and hugged Staley. The air raid sirens sounded in Chicago. Somewhere on the highway between Bloomington and Chicago a station wagon slid off the road, and Bill Veeck said, "The magic number is none!"

CHAPTER **2**

The White Sox Brass

THE FOUR DECADES of drought were ended. Those dismal second-division seasons, and disappointing second-place finishes, could be forgotten. The 1959 White Sox had finally brought the American League championship back to Chicago. And who would have thought it? Who would have believed that the White Sox, their front office torn by bitter dissension through most of this marvelous Go-Go era, would lead the pack in '59?

There were only a few. Manager Al Lopez, who steadfastly refused to concede. And Dick Dozer and this writer, both of the *Chicago Tribune*, who singled out the White Sox in preseason picks. A handful of others. Mainly, though, the experts had forecast 1959 as a year of decline for the White Sox. Fan interest, an amazingly accurate barometer, had indicated lack of confidence; and despite orders from the dedicated Old Guard regulars, ticket manager Tom Maloney greeted spring of 1959 by announcing that advance sales were far off. If the team failed, attendance might drop below the poor mark of '58, only 797,451. Instead, a miracle happened, and the all-time White Sox attendance mark was shattered.

Behind the amazing success sealed in Cleveland the night of September 22 were six rugged individualists:

Bill Veeck, former owner of the Milwaukee Brewers, Cleveland Indians, and St. Louis Browns, whose baseball apprenticeship was served under his father, then president of the Chicago Cubs.

Charles A. (Chuck) Comiskey, long impatient to seize full command of the baseball club that had been both a joy and a heartbreaking disappointment to his grandfather.

John Dungan Rigney, a most patient Irish gentleman who had starred as a White Sox pitcher and married Chuck's sister Dorothy.

Frank Lane, the volatile general manager who ushered in the Go-Go era.

Paul Rapier Richards, Lane's first Go-Go manager.

Alfonso Ramon (Al) Lopez, the long-time catching great who was to succeed where fifteen predecessors had failed.

Lesser roles were played by the late Mrs. Grace Comiskey, an iron-handed boss; Dorothy Comiskey Rigney, mother of two daughters; and Manager Marty Marion.

First must come William Veeck, Jr.

The season of 1958 was near the midway point the night that I was yanked into a Comiskey Park corner and told, "Find out why Bill Veeck came to Chicago from Cleveland today." There followed hours of frantic telephone calls, to the Chicago suburbs and Philadelphia and St. Louis and Cleveland, to check on Veeck's whereabouts. Shortly after 3 A.M., I located him back in Cleveland, where he maintained a partnership in a public relations business.

The former owner of the Indians and Browns coyly gave a business excuse for his hasty trip to Chicago. *Chicago Tribune* photographer Eddie Smith had reported that Butterfield Country Club scuttlebutt had the Rigneys willing to sell Dorothy's 54 per cent interest in the White Sox, but Veeck's explanation seemed plausible. Thought of his possible association with the White Sox was dismissed.

A few days later, the story broke. Veeck had made an offer

Little did Willie Veeck know then that one day he would hire and fire managers. Joe McCarthy was the Cub boss when Bill's heart was on the North Side.

for the Rigney shares in the White Sox. Interest died as the Rigneys pondered. Eventually, Veeck paid Dorothy Rigney $100 for an option to purchase her shares for $2,700,000, more or less. The fact that Veeck held the option was uncovered by Wilfrid Smith, sports editor of the *Chicago Tribune*, in late December of '58. Early in 1959, Veeck announced he would exercise the option.

Bill Veeck finally was coming home. He had been a long time coming.

Bill Veeck was born February 9, 1914, the youngest son of William Veeck, Sr., a sports writer who wrote under the pseudonym of "Bill Bailey." The senior Veeck's pen was as critical and barbed then as the junior Veeck's tongue was to become. He frequently was caustic about the Chicago Cubs. A sample: "My new son can throw his bottle farther than the team can hit." William Wrigley, Jr., the chewing gum magnate who owned the Cubs and was a rabid fan, soon suggested that the elder Veeck try his hand at operating the club and prove he was so smart. Veeck the elder shucked his sportswriting job and moved to the Cubs; no Veeck ever has been known to bypass a challenge. This brought young Bill on the baseball scene, too. As a youngster he would go with his father to Cubs Park and poke his nose into any open corner. Partially to keep the boy out of trouble, Veeck the elder saw that he had jobs with the ground crews and the concessionaires. During one long spell, later, young Bill was required to be at the park near 5 A.M. daily to ice up the goodies. This early rising became a habit, and many mornings in 1959 Bill would astound Comiskey Park personnel by popping into his office before 6 A.M.

Besides his first experiences with the Cubs, Bill had more formal schooling. He attended Hinsdale High School and was exposed to some football competition. There was a stretch at a swank but spartan ranch school at Los Alamos, New Mexico, later the birthplace of the atom bomb, where swimming and tennis and skiing were top sports. Another port of call was

Phillips Academy, which graduated him in 1932. Next came a year and a half at Kenyon College in Ohio, but his father's death, in the middle of the depression, left Bill on his own. He quit Kenyon, after making two promises to himself: that somehow he would continue his education; and that he would earn a living in baseball, where hard work seemed like play. Confidently, he offered himself to the Cubs for whatever exalted post needed his services. The Cubs studied Veeck's qualifications and found him most suited for the position of office boy, a capacity in which he had lost more than $10,000 worth of ticket orders for the 1929 World Series.

Veeck was to keep both promises. Mainly he was to earn his living in baseball, and in years to come a handsome living that saw him win a reputation as America's greatest check grabber. He also strove to continue his education, and took courses in architecture and accounting at Northwestern University and Lewis Institute. Later Bill turned to ranching and supervised his 47,000-acre New Mexico spread while studying law at night. Cowpokes accompanying him on jeep rides over the ranch found Veeck a poor conversationalist; he was too occupied spouting off law passages memorized during the previous evening's study.

If Veeck amazed with a capacity for study, he caused greater amazement with his talent for producing money, usually someone else's, out of thin air. In 1935, while honeymooning at French Lick, Indiana, with his first wife, he wired the Cubs: IF YOU WANT ME BACK, SEND MONEY. Of course the Cubs complied, and their brash boy Barnum was off again. The first Mrs. Veeck, a former elephant trainer, said, "When I married Bill, I thought I was through with circuses. I was wrong."

Veeck was rising in the Cubs' front office, but life seemed too tame. So in 1939, when the bank trustee for the estate of J. Louis Comiskey sought permission to sell the White Sox for protection of the heirs, he lined up financial backers and readied a bid for the club. Alas! His debut as Sox chieftain was delayed two decades as Mrs. Grace Comiskey, widow of J. Louis Comiskey, succeeded in thwarting the bank's move to sell the club.

By 1941, Bill was treasurer of the Cubs and more impatient. He learned that the Milwaukee Brewers' American Association franchise was available. Veeck's assets at the moment included $11 in cash, knowledge that Charlie Grimm had a loose $25,000 to invest, and nerve enough to ask other outside financing. He bought the Brewers, and a Horatio Alger story began. It did not begin auspiciously; the Brewers drew only twenty-two paid admissions the first day Veeck was on hand as boss. Quickly, though, as his dynamic personality captivated them, the Milwaukee burghers stormed the park. They were not coming to see good baseball, because in those days the patched-up Brewers played anything but good baseball. Fans did come in to see what new gimmicks Veeck would introduce to keep their minds off the game. This was the introduction of Veeck's philosophy that, while a baseball team might not give the fans a winner every day, it always could give them comfort and excitement in the park.

There were strange door prizes: pigeons, cakes of ice, live chickens. There were breakfast games for war workers, with some of the stadium personnel appearing in pajamas. German bands, too. A pitcher emerged from a giant cake during one pregame frolic. Best of all, there was Herr Charlie Grimm as manager. In 1942, Veeck's Brewers topped the minor leagues with an attendance of 273,589. His financial obligations were pared to $17.

Then, one night in New York, Bill Veeck met Barney Ross, the former boxing champion, who had gone to war with the Marines. Baseball life sounded boring after Ross's harrowing tales of South Pacific combat. Next thing, Milwaukee's baseball genius was in Marine garb.

In the South Pacific, Veeck had one big dream: advancement to the major leagues. He had weary hours to ponder this dream while hospitalized for a leg injury incurred during combat. In 1945, Veeck waived disability claims and headed for home. Subsequently, his leg was amputated below the knee, a handicap that failed to slow him down. Marty Caine, a Cleveland booking agent, has recalled: "I was with Veeck the night before the amputation, and you'd think he had nothing more on his mind than where he could find another pitcher. Then, shortly after he was outfitted with an artificial leg, Bill went out and danced most of the night. The pain, I'm certain, was terrific; he took a great chance of injuring himself permanently – of rendering the pain chronic – but he wanted to show us that he could take it."

Veeck could take it, all right, but there were those who couldn't when Barnum Bill, in the middle of routine conversation, would lift up a trouser leg and snuff out a cigarette stub on an ashtray built into the artificial member.

Bill Veeck, ex-Marine, reached baseball's big leagues on June 22, 1946: He became president and 30 per cent stockholder of the Cleveland Indians, and Cleveland was never the same. Neither were some of the old order, who resented his brashness and "commercialism." But Veeck quickly gave Cleveland a major league championship, its first since 1920. He also gave them stunts.

Tepees were pitched in the Indians' outfield. A supervised playroom was installed for small children. Bands, of course. Fireworks, too – Veeck loved fireworks. One close friend avowed that Bill's greatest unfulfilled ambition is to go back to the Chicago Cubs' hallowed old grounds and touch off $100,000 worth of skyrockets, pinwheels, and bombs, right in front of conservative Philip K. Wrigley, who gave Veeck temporary employment early in the 1950's but finally adjudged him incorrigible.

Cleveland, however, was thrilled with Veeck. Fans packed mammoth Municipal Stadium, 2,620,627 of them in the pennant year of '48 – a record that still stands. They thrilled at the hitting of Larry Doby, first Negro to play in the American League, and marveled at the pitching of Satchel Paige, the ageless barnstormer, who was signed with the help of Abe Saperstein, owner of the Harlem Globe Trotters. They cheered Manager Lou Boudreau, who had survived his troubles with Veeck. They giggled at gifts of nylons. They laughed at Veeck's flagpole sitter, and at the funeral service for the 1948 pennant when the Indians failed to repeat in 1949. Perhaps Veeck's most zany stunt was Good Old Joe Earley night. Good Old Joe Earley had written to a Cleveland newspaper protesting that the Indians had appreciation nights for almost everyone except the good old fans. Veeck responded so quickly one might have suspected that he had planted the letter.

On Good Old Joe Earley night, Good Old Joe was beckoned to home plate to receive an automobile, just as if he were a great major league star. Good Old Joe's automobile was a 1922 roadster! He also received a swayback horse — and a horse laugh from Mrs. Good Old Joe Earley, who wound up with a nifty new refrigerator and the latest model convertible.

Good Old Joe Earley night subsequently was topped, not in Cleveland but in St. Louis. Veeck had accepted the almost impossible task of revitalizing the Browns following his sale of the Cleveland Indians, a transaction necessary to complete a divorce settlement with the first Mrs. Bill Veeck. The St. Louis prank outraged baseball's conservatives.

It was a Sunday afternoon and the Browns were host to Detroit. As Detroit's Bob Cain prepared to pitch to the Browns' lead-off man, a pinch hitter was announced. Fans blinked in disbelief as Ed Gaedel, three feet seven inches tall, strode out with a tiny bat. Umpires tried to chase the midget, who then presented an official American League contract. Gaedel drew a walk from Detroit's infuriated pitcher, and Veeck an angry telegram from Will Harridge, then American League president: NO MORE MIDGETS!

Bill Veeck's introduction of a midget (the idea came from a James Thurber short story) was a success in St. Louis. Little

How many more worlds can Bill Veeck conquer?

else was. When August Busch, the millionaire brewer, purchased the St. Louis Cardinals, the Browns' National League rivals, Veeck knew his days were numbered. He said, "You can't fight that bankroll."

Veeck had to move, and he had been studying possible sites for the transfer of his franchise. He already had sized up the West Coast as a gold mine, although perhaps not yet ready to be exploited. He ached to go back to Milwaukee with a major league team, but Lou Perini's Boston Braves owned those territorial rights. So Veeck chose Baltimore. The setup was perfect: Baltimore wanted a major league team and the American League wanted Baltimore.

But the American League's brain trust included a few who wanted to get rid of the progressive young man who was embarrassing them by building good ball teams and radically entertaining fans. They squeezed Veeck out by holding up an okay on the switch to Baltimore. Without operating capital, Veeck had to sell the Browns. He did, at a profit. Then he sadly watched the American League approve the club's transfer.

Veeck vowed he would be back, someday. He failed in a bid to buy the Detroit Tigers. This was a disguised blessing, because Dorothy Comiskey Rigney was willing to listen when Veeck made his 1958 pitch for the Go-Go White Sox. When Mrs. Rigney agreed to the sale, Veeck was home free. There was nothing anyone in baseball could do about Veeck's purchasing Mrs. Rigney's 54 per cent stock interest. But Charles A. (Chuck) Comiskey, II, Mrs. Rigney's brother, would try. Chuck owned 46 per cent of the White Sox and he was going to battle Veeck as he had battled his mother and, later, his sister.

Chuck's maneuvering to wrest control of the White Sox was the one discordant note during the otherwise joyous season of 1959. The wrangle still was going on as 1959 passed into 1960, although with Veeck in the opposite corner the feuding was less bitter than Chuck's disagreement with his sister.

Charles A. Comiskey had two things in common with his antagonist. Both were descended from Chicago baseball families and both were strong-willed. Whatever has been said for and against them, if Bill Veeck had the right to grasp a sound investment opportunity when he saw it, then Chuck Comiskey had the right to fight for his own interests.

Bill Veeck was twelve years old when he first dreamed of owning a baseball club. At a much younger age, Chuck Comiskey was led to believe that he would someday inherit a baseball club, the Comiskey family's Chicago White Sox. This belief was fostered by a doting grandfather, Charles A. (the Old Roman) Comiskey, who had revolutionized play at first base, and been a standout manager with the old St. Louis Browns, before founding the Chicago White Sox and helping to found the American League. In an interview for A. M. (Mike) Kennedy, day managing editor of the *Chicago Tribune*, Chuck Comiskey once told me:

"My grandfather lived with us, and there was many a Sunday afternoon when little Charles had to be ushered away from his toys in the library so the men could settle down to playing pinochle and talking baseball. There were grandfather and my father — J. Louis Comiskey — and most always Commissioner Kenesaw Mountain Landis, who made a ritual of Sunday walks and breakfasts with Grandfather.

"And there'd be Leslie O'Connor, Landis's assistant, who was to succeed Harry Grabiner as general manager of the Sox. And Grabiner himself, and any of the top baseball people who happened to be in Chicago on those particular Sundays. I'd bet that many of the policies of baseball were settled right in that old, smoke-filled library of ours.

"I was the only grandson, so naturally the Old Roman doted on me. Often he would slip me a twenty-dollar bill. I had a baseball uniform when I was a year old — so they told me. Of course, one of my first toys was a football; probably my father's influence because he had played tackle at La Salle High School here in Chicago.

"There's not too much, though, that I remember about the Old Roman — I wasn't quite six when he died. I remember he talked about lots of the Sox, including Lew Fonseca, the first White Sox manager I can recall — although I have a picture showing me, a real little feller, with Ray Schalk when he was our manager.

"The White Sox were the most important thing in my grandfather's life — after his family — so it was natural he'd talk mostly about them. But one outside player he always raved about was Ty Cobb.

"While Grandfather was still alive, I got down to San Antonio with the White Sox on a spring training trip. What I remember about that is how tired my legs were when I went hiking with the players. When I'd get worn out, they'd park me along the road, continue on up some hill they were scaling, then pick me up on the way back.

"But while I was growing up I wasn't permitted to spend too much time in Comiskey Park. We had a farm up in Wisconsin, near Eagle River, and my sisters — Dorothy and Grace, who died in 1952 — and I spent most of our vacations there. All the young Comiskeys had chores. The girls would set the table and wash the dishes. Sometimes they pressured me into drying the plates. Later I drove a team of horses, and by that time I was playing baseball with summer teams in the area. This was after my father died.

"My grandfather had died at the farm in October of 1931, and my father took over control of the White Sox. In the summer of 1939, we were at the farm, and on July 4 the whole family was gathered. My father was ill at the time, but I didn't realize it, particularly when he took us over to the Fourth of July parade in Eagle River. As J. Louis Comiskey, he had a preferred parking spot. It was quite a celebration, and I got in the pie-eating contest. But I noticed my father wasn't as happy as he had been on lots of other visits to the farm. As I said, I didn't realize how sick he was. He died at the farm on July 18."

The Old Roman was dead. His son, J. Louis Comiskey, was dead. Now, in July of 1939, the next male in line was thirteen-year-old Chuck Comiskey. He was the heir apparent, because his mother, Grace Comiskey, was determined that the White Sox should not then pass from Comiskey hands.

In years to come, Chuck was to make several bids for control of the club. His first bid, though, was a comical one, and came not long after his father's death. The White Sox were entertaining Philadelphia at a Sunday session and a dispute arose when a Chicago player was called out on a close one. Chuck, just fourteen and wearing White Sox uniform No. 13, watched intently from the bench as Manager Jimmy Dykes tongue-lashed Umpire Johnny Quinn. Dykes was thumbed out by the umpire. Coaches Muddy Ruel and Mule Haas, who attempted to continue the argument, also were bounced.

Ted Lyons, the fabled Chicago pitcher and later manager of the White Sox, had an impish notion. He turned to young Chuck. "You're the owner of this ball club. Why don't you do something?"

In the stands, Mrs. Grace Comiskey gasped at the sight of Chuck resolutely striding out to the plate. En route, Chuck passed Dykes, who was headed for the bathhouse. Chuck paid no attention as Dykes roared, "Where the devil do you think you're going?"

Chuck reached Umpire Quinn, who snapped at Wally Moses of the Sox, "Now you've got the bat boy out here!"

"This is young Comiskey," said Moses. "He owns the team."

Ed Rommel, another umpire, seized Chuck and carried him to the bench with this admonition: "One more move and I'll turn you over my knee." To Lyons, Rommel added: "Another bright idea, and you'll be in the showers."

Whereas Bill Veeck's midget gag was responsible for President Will Harridge's edict against midgets, the Chuck Comiskey and Umpire Quinn incident prompted Harridge's suggestion that thereafter it would be better if young executives remained out of the dugouts during games.

During World War II Chuck served in the Navy, and later studied at St. Thomas (Minn.) College, where one year he batted .667 as a first baseman. His first serious attempt to take control of the White Sox came on the eve of the Go-Go era. Others were to follow. But Chuck was destined to have a strong voice in assembling the 1959 American League champions. Following the departure of Frank Lane and the death of Mrs. Comiskey, Chuck was the front man for the White Sox. Beside him was brother-in-law John Dungan Rigney.

John Dungan Rigney, born October 28, 1914, would have been a leading figure in any history of the Chicago White Sox even had he not married (in October of 1941) Dorothy Comiskey, eldest of the three children of J. Louis Comiskey. He spent eight seasons in a White Sox uniform, winning 64 and losing 64. After the 1947 season, his playing career curtailed by three seasons in the Navy and a service injury, he moved into the front office. There he was tops; and after Mrs. Rigney had sold her stock to Bill Veeck, he said forlornly, "Of course I'm going to miss all of this. You can't be a part of something for so long, and then pack up and leave, without missing it."

The Sox drove some almost unbelievable bargains, most of them engineered by Frank Lane, in obtaining player talent. But few paid more handsome dividends than the $1,000 that gained title to a good pitcher, a son-in-law, and a vice-president.

Here's how Johnny Rigney told me of the highlights of his playing days:

"When I graduated from St. Luke's parochial school, in River Forest, Illinois, in 1926, the class prophecy was that one day I'd be a star pitcher for the White Sox. I had started pitching in the sixth grade, and had been a White Sox fan even before that — largely through the influence of my father, who was a fanatic about the White Sox and Babe Ruth. We always were out in Comiskey Park when the Yankees came to town; my father rooted for the White Sox to win and Babe to hit a homer or two.

"After leaving St. Luke's, I went to St. Mel High School in Chicago. There my coach was Paddy Driscoll, a great Chicago athlete who had played briefly with the Cubs but who is more famous as a football player at Northwestern and with the Chicago Cardinals, and head coach of the Chicago Bears football team. It was a shock, in my sophomore year, when Driscoll cut me off the baseball team. I played basketball at St. Mel and continued in baseball as a pitcher on American Legion teams. Then at St. Thomas College in Minnesota I went out for both basketball and baseball. When summer came, I joined one of Chicago's famous semi-pro clubs, John Callahan's Logan Squares. Next summer I was back with the Logan Squares, and Clarence Rowland, a former White Sox manager who was then scouting for the Cubs, gave me a pep talk. Rowland had me talk to William Walker, the Cubs' president. The Cubs offered a chance with Ponca City, Oklahoma. When I said no thanks, they talked about a contract with their Los Angeles club.

"Then the Washington Senators wanted to take a look at me. The workout was to be in Comiskey Park, but the fellow at the gate refused to pass me in without a ticket. I went home.

"Finally a bid came from the White Sox. Maybe I didn't realize it at the moment, but it was what I had been waiting for, so I signed the Sox contract and they purchased me from Callahan. That was August of '34. Early in '35 I quit St. Thomas to go to spring training with the club. It was a trip I'll never forget.

"The train left Chicago in the evening, and I told all my West Side pals to meet it at the Oak Park station, where I'd talk to them from the observation platform. Well, when I got on the train, I was so lonesome I went to bed. Instead of me, the Oak Park gang found Al Simmons, and maybe George Earnshaw, on the observation platform. Simmons told 'em they had the wrong train, because there certainly was no one by the name of Johnny Rigney on the White Sox.

"That season I was a baseball hobo. The White Sox sent me to Dallas of the Texas League. Then I went to Albany and Des Moines. I became disgusted, collected my salary, and made a visit back to St. Thomas. I talked to Bob Connery of the St. Paul American Association team and he lined me up with Portsmouth. Portsmouth released me, and I went back to St. Paul. I played in thirty-two games for St. Paul, winning eight and losing four, but the White Sox didn't want me back, and St. Paul wasn't too enthused, either.

"St. Paul did offer me a conditional contract for '36. Apparently the winter's rest helped a sore arm that had been bothering me, because I had a fair season with St. Paul — thanks to lots of help from Manager Gabby Street. I won twelve and lost eleven, throwing a pretty fair fast ball with a good arm. The White Sox purchased me from St. Paul and I was with them in spring training in '37.

"I saw my first major league action on opening day of '37. The White Sox were in St. Louis and I came in as a reliever. I struck out Joe Vosmik, the first man I faced. I congratulated myself; big-league pitching was easy. The next batter was Rogers Hornsby, and he knocked me down with a long drive.

"Another game I'll never forget was on August 14, 1939. I pitched and won the first night game ever played in Comiskey Park.

"Then, in 1942, when I was with the Great Lakes Bluejackets, I pitched against the White Sox. At one point Jimmy Dykes, the White Sox manager, ordered Frank Pytlak purposely passed to get at me. I hit the second-longest home run I've ever seen in baseball.

"Let me tell you about the longest home run I ever saw. In 1941, Ted Williams got six homers off me, and everyone kidded about me being a soft touch for Williams. At Great Lakes, I was introduced as 'Ted's cousin.' It became tiresome, and I promised myself that after the war I'd throw Williams some pitches he couldn't even smell. Well, 1946 came, and I'm pitching against the Red Sox. I almost breeze a fast one by Williams. Well, right there came the longest home run I ever saw.

"Honestly, I can't say that Williams' homer was a surprise. Luke Appling, our shortstop, had asked me where I wanted him to play for Williams, and I had said, 'If I had my way, I'd put you in the right field stands.'

"Sure, I fed up lots of other home run balls. Frank Crosetti of the Yanks got one with the bases filled. Sam Chapman of the Athletics nearly sent me back to the minors with a home run blast in 1938. Just before I went into the Navy, Joe Di Maggio hit two homers off me. Then there was the time we were in Boston and I was rooming with Boob McNair. When McNair learned I was pitching this particular day, he said, 'Well, you don't have to worry about Jimmy Foxx. He and I were out a little late last night.'

"So the game starts, and I get the first two batters. This brings up Jimmy Foxx. Two fast balls give me two strikes on him. Then I decide to give him a change-up.

"Foxx smashed the pitch over the left field fence."

Rigney, who credits George Earnshaw as well as Gabby Street for polishing his pitching technique, won five and lost five in 1946, his first postwar season. In 1947, he won only two and lost three. A shoulder operation failed to correct his service injury, and Rigney traded his spot on the dugout bench for a swivel chair. He became the White Sox farm director and, on November 16, 1955, a vice-president. With Chuck Comiskey, previously appointed a vice-president, he shared the general manager's duties so long executed by Frank Lane. Glen Miller succeeded Rigney as farm director.

With Chuck Comiskey apparently the executive vice-president, Rigney attempted to remain in the background and avoid conflict with his brother-in-law. But with Chuck seeking to wrest control of the club from Dorothy Rigney, and remarks going the rounds that Rigney was more interested in the stock market quotations than in the box scores, relations were often strained. John remained calm and gracious. He took pride in the deals he helped make and in the youngsters he brought into the Go-Go organization. His baseball acumen was one reason the White Sox ascended to the championship in 1959, only a few months after Rigney had ceased to participate in club affairs. When he yielded his office chair to Bill Veeck, he yielded it with sadness but without fanfare.

Rigney never was one for fanfare. For example, late in the 1958 season, when speculation waxed hot about Al Lopez's retention as manager, Rigney proposed to end it at once. Between games, he and Comiskey went to the manager's bandbox office and asked Lopez if he would like to come back for '59.

"Yes, of course," said Al.

There were handshakes, then Comiskey and Rigney sent the news to the press box.

Alfonso Ramon (Al) Lopez, under whose genius and Castilian charm the Go-Go White Sox finally scaled the pennant peak, carried worthy credentials when he appeared in Chicago on October 30, 1956, as successor to the departing Sox skipper, Marty Marion. As an active player, Al had caught a major league record of 1,918 games, all but sixty-one of them in the National League. From the time he was a teenager in Tampa, Florida, until a fractured finger ended his big-league playing career in its seventeenth season, Al Lopez toiled behind the plate for many of the game's headline hurlers, from Walter Johnson to Van Lingle Mungo to Bob Feller.

Lopez's role as an iron man in the iron mask caused Ray

Berres, White Sox coach and a playing contemporary of Al's, to lament during 1957 spring training: "That Lopez kept the rest of us catchers poor men."

With a twinkle, Lopez responded: "Berres, it was your bat that kept you a poor man."

Al Lopez's debut as a big-league manager was delayed when plans went awry for Bill Veeck, then the flamboyant young owner of the Cleveland Indians. Veeck had intentions of trading off Lou Boudreau, his manager and star shortstop, for Vernon Stephens, the slugging shortstop of the St. Louis Browns; and Lopez was alerted to be ready to accept Boudreau's post. But Veeck failed to bring off the swap and Boudreau stayed on to enjoy a glorious, if sometimes turbulent, tenure as the heap big Injun chief. So Lopez could not command Cleveland's forces until the 1951 season, which found Boudreau playing for the Boston Red Sox.

By that time Lopez had three years of managing experience behind him. These had come with Indianapolis, which won the American Association pennant in 1948, Lopez's first season, and was second in both 1949 and 1950. The three-year stretch at Indianapolis established a pattern. Through 1959, in twelve seasons as manager at Indianapolis, Cleveland, and Chicago, Lopez never finished lower than second!

At Indianapolis, Lopez worked closely with Owen Joseph (Donie) Bush, old-time American League star infielder and White Sox manager in 1930 and 1931. The close friendship between Lopez and Bush was an inspiration to all who met them.

Lopez directed the Cleveland Indians from 1951 through 1956. Five times his club finished second to the Yankees, but in 1954 they were able to crash through to the pennant with 111 victories, an American League record. Lopez's World Series experience was a sad one. His Indians bowed to the New York Giants, four games to none.

Unrest settled on Cleveland in 1955. Lopez, a proud man, knew that someday he must go, and on the day before the final game of the 1956 season, he announced he was quitting. "I'm sorry I didn't do better," he said.

Henry (Hank) Greenberg, the former home run king who then was Cleveland's general manager, said Lopez's action was a surprise and disappointment. Actually, it was not much of a disappointment to big Hank, because he and Lopez had not been compatible. Ironically, the two were reunited in 1959, when Hank moved into the White Sox front office with Bill Veeck.

At the time Lopez made it clear that his woes with Greenberg were not serious enough to make him bitter. And he added, "After I resigned, Hank volunteered to try to get me another big-league manager's job. When it became apparent that the job he had in mind was going to someone within the organization, I shrugged. If nothing else turned up I would take my wife, Connie, and Al, Junior, to Europe for a year. I had saved my money and made some good investments, and I always had wanted to visit Spain, the birthplace of my father, and of my mother's folks.

"Then Chuck Comiskey telephoned and said that he and John Rigney and Roy Egan were agreed on me as the new White Sox manager. We talked that night, October 28, and again the next morning. I telegraphed my acceptance in the afternoon."

The talented young son of Modesto Lopez once said that had it not been for baseball, he most likely would have found his life's work in the Tampa cigar factories. That opinion, while typical of Lopez's humility, never was taken seriously by his many friends. A gentleman of Lopez's class and intelligence would have risen to prominence in any one of several fields.

Lopez had not reached his tenth birthday when he aspired to be a baseball catcher as skilled as two older brothers, who were considered great shakes on the sandlots around Ybor City, Tampa's Spanish settlement. When he was ten, came a temporary lapse in Al's catching career. He suffered a broken nose in a sandlot game — retribution, perhaps, for having played hooky from school.

"The kids thought I was killed and called an ambulance," Lopez told me. "I sneaked home from the hospital that night convinced of two things — that I was going to get a whipping, and that I was through with catching. At first I said I was through with baseball, but pretty soon I was back out there, pitching and playing shortstop. Then, a couple of years later, our school team faced a catching shortage, so I went behind the plate again. I stayed there."

Clark Griffith's Washington Senators were also short of catchers when they began spring training in Tampa in 1925. A Spanish newspaperman told them about Chico Al Lopez, a promising youngster of sixteen.

"Griffith talked to me and made it plain I'd only catch batting practice. No hitting, no fielding! Was I surprised when he offered $35 a week; I'd have caught for nothing. When the Senators were ready to leave Tampa, someone suggested I be taken north. But Griffith again made it plain the club wasn't interested in me. Anyhow, I'd already signed with the Class D Tampa club, in the Florida State League, for $150 a month. I was with Tampa for two seasons, then at Jacksonville and Macon before catching three games for Brooklyn in 1928. After a year at Atlanta I was back at Brooklyn to stay, and caught 128 games in 1930.

"I'm pretty proud of the record number of games I caught. I'm proud, too, of having caught Walter Johnson in an exhibition when I was just a kid, and of catching more than one hundred games for twelve seasons, of winning the pennant at Cleveland in 1954 and at Chicago in 1959."

Brooklyn obtained more than a first-class catcher when it paid Jacksonville $10,000 for Al Lopez. It also obtained a man who inspired his fellows, who was to become an outstanding leader — and one of baseball's finest storytellers.

For example, here's one Al tells on Walter "Boom-Boom" Beck:

"I was catching for Brooklyn in '34, with Casey Stengel managing and Hack Wilson in the outfield. We were playing the Phils in that old Baker Bowl in Philadelphia, and Beck was pitching. Well, Wilson and Beck were both having a bad time. You know that short right field fence, made of tin, in Baker Bowl, and the Phils were lining drives off it all afternoon. All you heard was *boom*, and then you saw a line drive caroming off the tin and Wilson waddling after it. *Boom, boom!* Poor old Hack — he should have caught at least some of 'em.

"Finally Stengel decided to yank Beck. Now it was my job in those days to tell the pitcher when he was through, but I saw Beck was boiling, so I didn't say much. Then Beck saw Wilson lying on the outfield grass — taking a rest while we huddled. Beck was so mad he wheeled and heaved the ball at Wilson like a shot from a cannon.

"Well, the ball hit the tin wall, and *boom*, it caromed off. Wilson jumped up, ran after the ball, and pegged it into second. Beck got so mad he kicked over a water bucket.

"Then Stengel said, 'That's fine, Walter. Now I can suspend you instead of selling you. If you'd had as much stuff on your pitches as on that one you let go at Wilson, you'd still be in there.' "

Lopez never tells any of his stories without warm affection for the principals involved. The same affection carries over in his dealing with broadcasters, sports writers, players, and coaches. His patient, quiet nature inspired the *Chicago Tribune*'s Edward Prell to write, "Lopez could even get along with Frank Lane."

Prell was referring to the same Frank C. Lane who, coming in as general manager at the birth of the Go-Go era, may have been the most colorful and explosive personality ever to operate in Comiskey Park. Certainly he is the most controversial.

Lane's appointment as general manager of the White Sox was announced in Cleveland on October 9, 1948, by Chuck

Comiskey. Lane replaced Leslie O'Connor, previously secretary to Commissioner Kenesaw Mountain Landis and later president of the Pacific Coast League. Lane masterminded the front office through seven turbulent seasons, surviving a short feud with his inherited manager, John (Honest John) Onslow, and Chuck Comiskey's walkout to Texas, before Mrs. Grace Comiskey released him from his contract — which had five years to run — in late September of 1955. During that span Lane became baseball's greatest trader, and negotiated 241 player deals.

Always outspoken, giving criticism and approbation as he felt they were deserved, Lane sometimes made his remarks a little too gamy for the Ladies' Aid. One such outburst led to the final break. In the end it was a long and bitter difference of opinion with young Chuck, his one-time ally, that brought about Lane's departure from the White Sox.

Frank Charles Lane, baseball's man of perpetual motion, was born in Cincinnati on February 1, 1896, the son of a druggist. Frank was ten when his father died. The family returned from Detroit to Cincinnati, and Frank found part-time work around a drugstore. The job paid $2.50 a week, plus all the ice cream Frank could eat. Ice cream became his regular breakfast.

When outside work did not interfere, Lane played high school football. He very soon was playing professional football, too. First there was the semi-pro brand, on the sandlots. Then, at eighteen, he became a lineman with the Cincinnati Celts. An added duty with the Celts was to help distribute the gate receipts among the players. From that early training, Frank Lane became dedicated to the belief that he should have a cut of the gate swag when attendance was great, and this led to healthy pay checks with the White Sox and, later, with Cleveland.

For two years, more or less, Lane studied law. His pro

football play found him moving from the Celts to the Dayton Triangles and Detroit Heralds. His baseball ambitions were thwarted by inability to hit a curve. Briefly, there was a $15-a-week job as sports editor of the *Cincinnati Commercial Tribune*. Lane was not much of a sports editor, but then the *Commercial Tribune* was not much of a newspaper.

Through the years Frank remained a physical fitness fanatic. He never smoked and seldom took even a sociable glass of wine. He began each day with calisthenics, and he still does.

Soon Frank went into sports officiating, and became an outstanding collegiate football and basketball whistle-tooter. The Lane trademark was a short-sleeved shirt that showed his bulging muscles to best advantage. Ed (Moose) Krause, now Notre Dame's athletic director, tells of a game he played for the Notre Dame basketball team at Pittsburgh. The crowd grew ugly as the Irish gave Pitt a roughing up, and then a Pitt player drew an especially violent foul.

"The fans stormed from the stands," recalls Krause, "and I was worried. But Lane stepped in front of me, his muscles bulging, and whacked the ringleader right on the kisser. That ended the riot."

Football officiating, strangely enough, led Lane to his career as a baseball executive. It was during a game that he made the acquaintance of another official – Larry MacPhail. MacPhail used Lane's friendship with a Cincinnati banker to engineer the deal in which industrialist Powel Crosley assumed control of the Reds in 1933. MacPhail went in as the top working executive and insisted that Lane also join the Reds' organization. This gave Frank an opportunity to learn the operation of a major league club from the ground up.

"In those days money was tight and we didn't have a half dozen in our office," Frank recalls. "I had several jobs – publicity, selling tickets, road secretary, sometimes janitor, too."

During his service as road secretary, Lane was approached by a hotel clerk who said, "Sir, your team may not have had much success, but I want to say that you can be proud of those boys. We've never had a better-behaved bunch of ballplayers in this hotel."

Lane's response: "Yes, and I'd rather have a bunch of cut-ups who'd win us some ball games."

At Cincinnati, Lane studied the MacPhail flair for promotion, saw Larry introduce night baseball to the major leagues in 1935. Lane remained with the Reds when MacPhail moved on, and was full-fledged farm director from 1937 through 1941. Things were looking up in Cincinnati, of course; the club won National League pennants in 1939 and 1940, and the 1940 World Championship.

World War II took Lane from the Reds. He went into the Navy as a lieutenant and emerged, in 1946, as a commander. Awaiting him upon discharge was a job offer from MacPhail — in the New York Yankee organization. Before the year was over, Lane left the Yankees to become president of the American Association. From that post he stepped into the White Sox front office.

Only a few days before young Chuck Comiskey hired Lane, he had signed a new field manager to replace Ted Lyons, the former pitching hero who had replaced Jimmy Dykes as skipper on May 25, 1946. The White Sox had been floundering under Lyons' management and, somewhat reluctantly, the Comiskey family decided that Ted would have to go. Chuck, who had returned to the White Sox in mid-season of 1948 after a brief stint in the farm system, made the announcement on October 3: Lyons was to be succeeded by Jack Onslow.

Onslow's baseball career had begun with Dallas in 1909. He had caught forty major league games, with the Tigers in 1912 and the Giants in 1917. His first managerial experience had been at Richmond, Virginia, in 1924. Onslow later was with the Pittsburgh, Washington, St. Louis, Red Sox, and Braves organizations. He joined the White Sox in 1946 as a scout, and was a coach when the team went to spring training in 1947. That season he became manager at Chicago's Waterloo farm and saw his team win the Three-I League play-offs. Onslow directed Memphis to second place in the Southern Association in 1948. He was almost sixty when the summons came from the Comiskeys.

Most of the writers and fans liked Onslow, and respected him. Honest John, however, had a mind of his own and was not about to budge for Lane. Nor would he take any of Lane's talk. Earl Flora, the Columbus, Ohio, sports editor who was Lane's publicity chief during the early days at Chicago, wrote in Herb Simons' *Baseball Digest* of a typical exchange between the two.

Thrusting out his jaw, Lane bellowed, "I could coach third base blindfolded better than you did this afternoon."

Honest John responded, "I don't doubt it. You do everything else blindfolded."

The 1949 White Sox rose to sixth place under Onslow. But Lane was after Honest John's job, intending to replace him with Paul Richards, then a promising minor league skipper. The Comiskeys backed Onslow, but Lane's rebuff was only a temporary one. Onslow got the ax early in the 1950 season, and for the balance of that campaign the club was under direction of John Michael (Red) Corriden, a graybeard born in Logansport, Indiana, on September 4, 1887. Corriden, who died while watching a telecast of the 1959 World Series, was only a stopgap pilot. Lane had Paul Rapier Richards waiting in the wings.

Lane and Richards were to become a storied team. So were the White Sox.

On October 10, 1950, Richards was named to succeed Corriden, who had been reluctant to step into friend John's shoes the previous May. Chicagoans did not know quite what to make of the news, and one newspaper pointed out that Richards was the fifth manager — Dykes, Lyons, Onslow, Corriden, and Richards — for the White Sox since early in 1946.

Richards, not yet tabbed as a hot-shot, came in with a mixed managerial record. He had won two Southern Association pennants with Atlanta and a single pennant in three seasons at Buffalo. His 1950 Seattle team had wound up sixth in the Pacific Coast League.

Richards, born November 21, 1908, in Waxahachie, Texas, attracted national attention while still playing high school baseball. The entire high school team had attracted national attention, in fact, by ringing up sixty-five consecutive victories. The team included such gents as Belvedere Bean, Art Shires, Jimmy Adair, and young Mr. Richards, an ambidextrous pitcher who had accomplished the believe-it-or-not feat of winning the first game of a doubleheader as a right-hander, and the second as a lefty.

Richards was sixteen when Nap Rucker signed him to a Brooklyn contract. Uncle Wilbert Robinson, the Brooks' eccentric manager, took one glance at the ambidextrous young pitcher and sent him to the Eastern Shore League. There young Richards' debut in organized baseball was marked by a contretemps in which the Waxahachie whiz whacked his manager on the chops.

Minor league wanderings took young Richards, then working as an infielder, to such diverse points as Crisfield, Waterbury, Muskogee, Macon and, finally, Asheville. Meanwhile, he had been drafted by the Browns and subsequently reclaimed by Brooklyn. It was back at Macon, in 1930, that Richards became a catcher.

Macon was managed by Charley Moore, who also was the catcher. No relief was on hand when Moore was injured. Richards volunteered. Paul caught on fast, and held the post after Moore recovered.

Brooklyn called the apprentice catcher up for a trial in 1932. Alas, he was no threat to the young incumbent, Al Lopez. His total employment at Brooklyn was three games. The New York Giants took title to him in 1933, and although overshadowed by the very able Gus Mancuso, Richards did put in more than two seasons in Giant flannels and caught the great Carl Hubbell. Following an injury to his throwing arm early in 1935, Richards was sold to the Athletics and worked eighty-five games. He next was sold to the Atlanta Crackers, for whom he caught, occasionally played first base, and, for five seasons, served as manager.

The wartime year of 1943 found Paul Richards back in the majors, this time at Detroit, where he had been hired as a coach by Manager Steve O'Neill. When Detroit's catching ran short, O'Neill called on the old war horse. Richards caught at Detroit from 1943 through 1946, and batted in six runs in the 1945 World Series victory over the Chicago Cubs.

His return to the managerial wars came at Buffalo, in 1947. From then on, it was up and up for Paul Rapier Richards.

As freshman manager at Chicago in 1951, Richards amazed the baseball world. His Go-Go White Sox had a long stretch in first place, finally finished fourth, highest since 1943, and drew 1,328,234 customers, an all-time attendance mark until the championship season of 1959.

Richards' Go-Go White Sox were third in 1952, 1953, and 1954. Then he gave in to overtures from Baltimore.

This left the Go-Go White Sox under the field leadership of Marty Marion, the immortal Cardinal shortstop and short-term pilot of the St. Louis Browns. Marion was to be with the club longer than General Manager Lane. Frantic Frank did not know it at the time, but when Richards left for Baltimore Lane had only another year to go with the White Sox.

The 1955 White Sox started well under Marion. A pennant looked possible. In mid-season Lane announced that Marty's contract had been extended through 1956. Not long there-after — late in September, following an outburst of trouble in the front office — Frank Lane offered his resignation. It was accepted by baseball's first lady, Mrs. Grace Comiskey.

Front office control was then taken over by Charles (Chuck) Comiskey and his brother-in-law, John Dungan Rigney. But behind the scenes, as she had been for so many seasons, was Grace Comiskey.

Mrs. Grace Reidy Comiskey, sixty-two-year-old widow of
J. Louis and president of the Chicago White Sox since 1941,
died at her breakfast coffee on December 10, 1956. That evening the late Roy Egan, the club's veteran attorney, recalled:

"From the time of her marriage to J. Louis Comiskey, the
White Sox were a great part of her life. For years the Comiskeys lived with the Old Roman, so she constantly was exposed to talk of the family ball team. Living in this baseball
atmosphere she built up a wonderful background for the day
when the burden of operating the White Sox fell to her.

"I remember when the Orioles and Yankees made the big
trade involving Don Larsen, Bob Turley, and Billy Hunter.
She immediately told me that the Yankees had come out
ahead.

"To Mrs. Comiskey it was inconceivable that any name
except that of Comiskey be associated with the Sox. That's
why she put up such a battle, after the death of her husband,
to prevent bankers from selling the club to solve estate problems. She had to borrow money to complete the battle, you
know. In recent years, when I received feelers asking if the
Comiskeys might consider selling the White Sox for a good
price, I answered that there just wasn't a chance.

"Mrs. Comiskey was a strong booster of the Chicago Cubs,
too. She considered competition from the Cubs a healthy
situation, a stimulus. And late last season, while Phil Wrigley
and his executives were getting some rough treatment in the
newspapers, she felt the criticism was unjust — she believed
Wrigley was sincerely trying to develop a winner. Sometimes, too, she felt that criticism of the White Sox was un-
fair, because she was trying her best, but criticism didn't
annoy her. She knew criticism was part of this business.

"Mrs. Comiskey had great ability to delegate authority;
she seldom interfered, never second-guessed. If some big
money had to be put out, or a player deal made, she relied on
the judgment of those hired to do the job. She followed the

baseball stories and the columnists; she was a constant reader of *The Sporting News*. She asked many keen questions and developed her own opinions. She didn't think that paying bonuses to unproven players was sound business; still, she was practical enough to go along when the Sox had to put up money to land a bonus player.

"Her greatest dream, of course, was to win an American League pennant for Chicago. Her hopes were high in 1955, and she made World Series plans.

"Yes, she had favorites. At the baseball writers' dinners she especially enjoyed visiting with Red Faber, Ray Schalk, and Joe Benz. Ted Lyons was another; he was the apple of her eye. And she was fond of Jimmy Dykes.

"On the Go-Go White Sox she admired Nellie Fox and Billy Pierce. She took quite a liking to Lu Aparicio in his rookie season."

Mrs. Comiskey had bristled like a mother hen when the bank trustee of her husband's estate had sought court permission to sell the White Sox to protect the value of the estate. In a brilliant coup engineered by her attorneys, Thomas J. Sheehan and Egan, Mrs. Comiskey renounced her husband's will to take her dower rights. The bank trustee, which had been seeking to protect itself as well as the Comiskeys, was given court permission to resign. Control was returned fully to the Comiskeys early in 1941.

Through the years, the belief grew that Mrs. Comiskey was saving the White Sox for her son, youngest of the three children. There seemed to be confirmation in the will of J. Louis Comiskey, which had expressed a desire that no White Sox stock be sold until Chuck was thirty-five. This belief persisted despite the differences between mother and son.

One person who did not subscribe to that belief was Frank C. Lane. Frantic Frank confided that Chuck would not inherit control of the White Sox. Whether he was indulging in wishful thinking or actually forecasting that majority ownership was to pass to Mrs. Dorothy Comiskey Rigney, he was right.

Mrs. Dorothy Comiskey Rigney, who much preferred the role of housewife and mother, ceased playing an unobtrusive role in the White Sox dynasty on December 21, 1956. That day she became a sports page headliner. The reading of Mrs. Grace Comiskey's will revealed that control of the Chicago American League baseball club had passed to her daughter Dorothy rather than to her son Chuck. By specifically bequeathing five hundred shares to Dorothy before the residue of the shares was divided evenly between brother and sister, Mrs. Comiskey ensured that Dorothy would be 54 per cent owner.

This was a bitter reverse to Chuck, but he made a gracious statement. It ended:

"The management of the White Sox will continue under the direction of Vice-Presidents Comiskey and Rigney. Charles Comiskey and Mrs. Rigney have decided, out of respect for Mrs. Comiskey's memory, that the office of president will remain vacant for at least a year."

Mrs. Rigney added, "There will be no changes. Charles and John will continue to run the ball club together just as they have. The influence I will exert will be behind the scenes, just as it always has been."

Mrs. Rigney's statement reflected more of a hope than a fact. There were to be changes — dynamic ones.

Before Mrs. Comiskey's will was read, Chuck and Dorothy each had 1,694 of the club's 7,450 capital shares. This total of 3,388 had passed to them from the estate of their father, J. Louis Comiskey. Dorothy now owned hers outright. One-third of Chuck's were to remain in trust until he reached his thirty-fifth birthday, November 18, 1960.

Mrs. Comiskey's shares, from her husband's estate and the estate of her other daughter, Grace Lou, totaled 4,062. After Dorothy's 500 came off the top, Chuck and Dorothy were to split evenly the remaining 3,562. Twice, in years to follow, the number of capital shares was to be reduced by retirement. But the change in the number of shares meant little. Ownership was to continue to be split 54 per cent to 46 per cent — at least through 1959.

Dorothy Rigney, who once played first base on the girls' team at St. Philip Neri grammar school on Chicago's South Side, first sat in on White Sox games when she was five years old. By that time she had been thoroughly indoctrinated in baseball lore, and particularly White Sox lore, by her grandfather and father. In 1937 she entered the front office as secretary to her father, J. Louis. She became club treasurer after his death and retained that post until selling her 54 per cent to the Veeck syndicate.

Like her mother, Mrs. Rigney was a confirmed sports fan. Many days she would be at Comiskey Park from 10:30 A.M. until 4:30 or 5 P.M. Then she would drive to the Rigney home in suburban River Forest to cook dinner for Johnny and their daughters, Mary Sharon, born in 1943, and Patti, born in 1948. Visitors found her a gracious hostess, and she was quick to invite a visitor to share a drink or a dinner.

Clearly Mrs. Rigney hoped that her husband and her brother would work together to guide the White Sox back to the glories that were the Old Roman's. Dorothy was content to let Chuck appear as family spokesman, and was happy to learn he was to be profiled in a *Chicago Tribune* series, and in Herb Simons' *Baseball Digest*. She scouted up pictures of Chuck to illustrate the articles.

A breach was to develop, however, and Dorothy finally asserted herself on December 18, 1957, after Chuck had suggested that she was the "victim of bad advice." In a prepared statement Dorothy countered Chuck's suggestion with considerable heat and several of her own; and in a review of the long family struggle for control of the club she left no doubt as to where she stood.

Weary of the interminable wrangling, realizing finally that

a baseball club was not a gilt-edged legacy to pass on to her two daughters, Dorothy Comiskey Rigney was in a mood to listen when Bill Veeck made his rush trip from Cleveland to Chicago a few months later.

The dynasty of the Old Roman was drawing to a close.

CHAPTER 3

As It Was
in the Beginning

CHARLES ALBERT COMISKEY, born in Chicago on August 19, 1859, entered the Hall of Fame, in Cooperstown, New York, with credentials as worthy as any of the baseball immortals enshrined there. The Old Roman was a notable first baseman who revolutionized play at his station. He was a storied manager at an age that finds most modern players at the height of their playing careers. He was also founder and owner of the Chicago White Sox, and an imposing and controversial figure.

There are those who would tarnish the esteem in which the father of the White Sox is held. They say that Commy, the first to pay the tab and provide lavish spreads for his players, was the last to pay them fair salaries. They say, "Commy always was buying new suits for the sports writers — and cutting the salaries of his players." And, "Comiskey liked to be a big shot with the crowd, but he was cheap with his players and that's why some of them turned into Black Sox."

If his critics are right, they should remember that the Old Roman did harsh penance. He died with a broken heart.

I prefer to think of Charles Albert Comiskey as Paul Caspers, a husky Chicago real estate man, portrayed him to me one evening in Red McNamara's, with such as Lieutenant Jim Hagerty, Lieutenant Al Noonan, Judge Dan McNamara, and Rog Whalen sitting around. Caspers came up to me and said, "You don't know me, but I know you. You're the guy who picked the White Sox to win the pennant. You don't know the hope you gave us. Unless you've lived in this neighborhood all of your life, you don't know what the White Sox can mean to people. Do you know that I go back before the champions of '17 — the Pants Rowland team? Let me tell you.

"We were neighbors of the Old Roman, and as far back as I can remember, my father was taking me to White Sox games. Sometimes we'd get in on passes; other times . . . well, it didn't cost much in those days. Yeh, I've been a White Sox fan since I can remember.

"One day — I was just a little kid — I got sick. I was really sick, lying in bed quiet as a corpse. They knew I was going to die, but a fellow who had gone to medical school with my father was using a serum, and they got him to rush to Chicago, and I was inoculated.

"The next day, the Old Roman learned I was sick and came to our house with a brand-new White Sox baseball. He talked to me, and all I could do was turn the baseball in my fingers. That baseball was the greatest thing that ever happened to me. The owner of the White Sox had given me a baseball! I was smiling when he left."

Charles A. Comiskey was relegated to a baseball career on a summer day in 1876. Young Commy was driving a wagon-load of bricks to the site of Chicago's new city hall, being built to replace the edifice destroyed in the Great Fire. En route, he stopped to pitch in a sandlot baseball game. He still was pitching when his father, Alderman John (Honest John) Comiskey, arrived on the scene. The elder Comiskey grabbed the reins and headed off, in disgust: his son deserved no better than to be a ballplayer.

According to G. W. Axelson, Comiskey's first Boswell,

the young Old Roman graduated from the 1876 sandlots. When his pitching arm gave him trouble, he switched to third base and, finally, to first. Eventually, after kicking around on informal teams, he found himself on the St. Louis Browns, which were owned, operated, directed, and controlled by "der boss president," Christopher Von der Ahe. In 1882, his first season with the Browns, Comiskey lost one pitching decision but made a favorable impression as a first baseman. In 1883, he managed the team and played first and the outfield. In 1884, he was first baseman only. He again was playing manager from 1885 through 1889.

As a player, Comiskey quickly revolutionized the style of play for first basemen by roaming far off the bag. Before him, first-sackers stayed on the base, and the balls whizzing beyond reach were the responsibility of other defenders. He became one of the first exponents of the head-first slide, reasoning that it enabled the runner to keep an eye on the base ahead and eliminated the possibility of a broken leg.

As a manager, Comiskey passed his first major milestone in 1885, when he piloted der boss president's team to the American Association championship. On October 14 began the interleague play-off with Adrian C. Anson's Chicago White Stockings, champions of the mighty National League. An estimated 3,000 saw the Browns and mighty Chicagos battle to an eight-inning draw, 5–5. Anson's White Stockings, all established old pros, fell victim of the jitters. They committed eleven errors and salvaged the deadlock only by an eighth-inning rally that produced four runs just before darkness moved in.

The teams then rushed to St. Louis for a second game on the following day. The Browns hit the White Stockings with a three spot in the first inning, but trailed by a 5–4 margin in the sixth when Manager Comiskey ordered his athletes from the field in protest of a decision by Umpire Dan Sullivan. This move cost the Browns a 9–0 forfeit loss, but Sullivan was relieved of further employment in the Series.

St. Louis won the third, 7–4, and the fourth, 3–2. Manager Comiskey's enthusiasm waned, however, as Chicago won the fifth game in Pittsburgh and the sixth in Cincinnati. Counting the forfeit, Anson's team now enjoyed a three-to-two edge in games. The seventh game also was played in Cincinnati and Comiskey's Browns rapped Chicago, 13–4. By most counts, the Series ended in a deadlock, three games to three, with the single draw, but Von der Ahe believed otherwise. He argued that the forfeited game should not count as a Chicago victory.

Comiskey's 1885 Browns had only Von der Ahe's boast to back up their claim to the World Championship. Comiskey's 1886 Browns had more. They walloped Anson's White Stockings, four games to two, in the '86 interleague play-off. At twenty-seven, Charles Albert Comiskey had directed a team to baseball's pinnacle, such as it was.

Comiskey's 1887 team champions lost to Detroit, ten games to five, in a marathon series that saw games in St. Louis, Detroit, Pittsburgh, Brooklyn, New York, Philadelphia, Boston, Washington, Baltimore, and St. Louis. The 1888 Series also was disastrous; Comiskey's Browns fell to the New York Giants, six games to four.

Comiskey's association with the Browns, who had paid him as much as $8,000 per year, was interrupted following the 1889 campaign. In 1890, Comiskey became manager of the Chicago entry in the short-lived Players' League, which attempted the sad experiment of abandoning the reserve clause. The Players' League lasted only one season, and 1891 found Comiskey back with Von der Ahe's American Association Browns. However, competition with the Players' League had weakened the old Association, and it folded after '91.

This sent Comiskey to Cincinnati as manager of that city's National League team. There he renewed acquaintance with a sports writer named Byron Bancroft (Ban) Johnson. A strong friendship developed which was to have a resounding impact on Organized Baseball. Sports writer Ban Johnson and Charles Albert Comiskey invented the American League.

The American League evolved from the old Western League, which on Comiskey's recommendation named Johnson president in 1894. Comiskey continued to lead Cincinnati's National League representative through 1894, then bought the Western League's Sioux City (Iowa) franchise and moved it to St. Paul. For four seasons Comiskey made futile bids for success at St. Paul. He played, managed, and handled the business affairs, but had no winner either on the field or at the box office. And all the while he kept a keen eye on Chicago.

In 1900, despite the misgivings of James A. Hart, owner of the Chicago National League franchise, Comiskey transferred his St. Paul franchise to Chicago's South Side. Hart finally agreed to this invasion by a minor league rival but drove a tough bargain. He won agreement that the Comiskey team would not play north of Thirty-fifth Street, and he restricted it from using "Chicago" in its name.

Then Johnson changed the Western's name to American League!

Comiskey, denied use of "Chicago," reactivated Cap Anson's old team nickname, White Stockings. The ancient and honorable nickname kindled fond memories for some of the older Chicagoans. It helped establish the team's identity with a city that already had a great baseball heritage.

The first part of the battle of Chicago was not an easy one. Comiskey even came to the point of declaring that he might abandon baseball and join the Windy City's police force. He had to borrow money to build a ball park on Thirty-fifth Street between Princeton and Wentworth avenues. Aside from his reputation as a baseball executive, aside from his Chicago family name, Comiskey had little to offer in the way of collateral.

But he got the money, some by loan and some by sale of stock. The ball park was completed in a feverish rush. Finally, with Manager Comiskey at the helm, the White Stockings took the field for their Chicago debut on April 21, 1900. A crowd in excess of 5,000 saw the inaugural battle against Connie Mack's Milwaukee club. Milwaukee won in ten innings, 5–4.

That opening-game defeat was one of only fifty-three sustained during regular season play. The White Sox soared to eighty-two victories to win the American League's first pennant. But no one paid much attention.

Recognition came the following year, when the American League realigned itself and expanded to the east. The 1901 American League line-up included Chicago, Milwaukee, Cleveland, and Detroit, four holdovers from 1900, plus four newcomers — Baltimore, Washington, Boston, and the Philadelphia Athletics. The 1900 contenders that had fallen by the wayside were Kansas City, Indianapolis, Buffalo, and Minneapolis.

The first game in official American League history was played in Comiskey's Chicago South Side ball park on April 24, 1901. An overflow crowd of more than 14,000 watched the duel with Cleveland. Owner Comiskey no longer was field leader; that post was held by a thirty-one-year-old right-handed pitcher pirated from Hart's Chicago National League team — Clark Calvin Griffith.

Manager Griffith assigned opening-game hurling chores to right-hander Roy (Boy Wonder) Patterson. The Boy Wonder held Cleveland to seven hits: White Sox 8; Cleveland, 2! The team was off and running.

Other Chicago participants in that game were catcher William J. (Billy) Sullivan, twenty-six; first baseman William Frank (Bald Eagle) Isbell, twenty-five; second baseman David L. Brain, twenty-four; third baseman Frederick Orrin (Dutch) Hartman, thirty-two; shortstop William Frank Shugart, thirty-three, a native Chicagoan; left fielder Samuel Blair (Sandow) Mertes, twenty-eight; center fielder William Ellsworth (Dummy) Hoy, thirty-eight; and, in right field, a twenty-six-year-old with the appropriate name of Fielder Allison Jones. Fielder Jones, who was destined to guide the White Sox to their first World Championship a few years hence, scored two runs — as did Shugart and Mertes — on that glorious opening day.

Jones topped the hitters with .325 as the White Sox went on to their first big-league pennant. Griffith's pitching arm accounted for twenty-four of the season's eighty-three victories. Fifteen victories were won by James Joseph (Jimmy) Callahan, a right-hander destined for important assignment in the Comiskey empire. Callahan, like Griffith and Mertes, had played with Hart's West Side Cubs the previous season. Their presence in the White Sox line-up made it clear that the upstart American League was a serious challenge to the long-established Nationals.

In 1902, the White Sox fell to fourth as Connie Mack's Athletics claimed the flag. St. Louis, a replacement for Milwaukee, finished second. Boston was third.

Baltimore's franchise was transferred to New York for 1903. Now the American League had a beachhead in the big time, and the National League was willing to call a truce. Chicago's Clark Griffith went to New York as manager. He was replaced in Chicago by Callahan, who on September 20, 1902, had pitched the White Sox's first no-hitter against Detroit.

The season of 1903 was a great one for the American League as a whole. Not only was New York invaded, but the Boston Red Sox defeated Pittsburgh, five games to three, in the first modern World Series. For the White Sox, however, the season was a dismal one; they skidded to seventh.

Now, with interleague peace established, the way was clear for a postseason series between the South Side White Sox and West Side Cubs. The Windy City rivals battled through fourteen games, each winning seven. The Cubs, runners-up in the National League, spurned Comiskey's challenge for a fifteenth and "rubber" match. The series left Comiskey fuming at the Cubs, but enthused about the prospects of a young left-handed pitcher named Nick Altrock. Nick had won only four regular season games but proved the White Sox stopper in the series with the Cubs. Comiskey was right: Altrock, later to become a professional baseball clown, won nineteen or more games in each of the following three campaigns, and in 1906 became the first White Sox pitcher ever to win a World Series game.

Fielder Jones replaced Callahan, who accepted a post in the outfield, as manager during the 1904 campaign. The White Sox finished third. They moved to second in 1905 as Altrock won 24, Frank (Yip) Owen won 22, and Frank Elmer Smith won 19, including a 15–0 no-hitter over Detroit on September 6.

Now Fielder Jones' greatest moment was at hand. It was the season of 1906, and for Chicago South Siders the greatest year in baseball. The White Sox not only regained the pennant, but turned back the Cubs in an All-Chicago World Series.

What a World Series that was!

CHAPTER 4

The Hitless Wonders

WHITE SOX VERSUS CUBS!

Chicago's dream-world Series was set to open on the West Side on October 9, 1906. Manager Frank L. Chance's Cubs, winners of an unprecedented 116 games while breezing to the National League championship, were top-heavy favorites. It was easy to understand why.

The Cubs had hitting. They had one of the game's best infields in first baseman Chance, second baseman Johnny Evers, shortstop Joe Tinker, and third baseman Harry Steinfeldt. Pitching? The Cubs had that, too: Mordecai Brown, the three-fingered wizard who had won 26 and lost 6; Big Ed Reulbach, who had won 19 and lost 4; lefty John Theodore Joseph Pfiester (Pfiestenberger), with 20–8; and Orval Overall, who had won 12 and lost 3 after arriving from Cincinnati.

Since Frank Isbell's .279 had paced Comiskey's "hitless wonders" to the 93 victories that had won the American League championship, clearly the White Sox were not going to murder the West Siders with power. But the Sox did have some potent pitching to counter the Cubs'. They had Frank (Yip) Owen, who in three seasons had won 65 games. They had Nick Altrock, a 20-game winner in 1906 regular season play, and Guy Harris (Doc) White, the lefty who had won 18. And they had a big, handsome right-hander who was just beginning to master the spitball picked up from Elmer G. Stricklett in spring training of 1904. The handsome young right-hander was Edward Augustin Walsh. He had won 17 decisions during the race to the pennant, 10 of them shutouts, three of them one-hitters.

With this pitching, and the spirit that had won 19 consecutive games during the regular season, the White Sox invaded the Cubs' West Side lair for the World Series opener. Snow flurries were coming down as the Cubs' Brown had his first pitch to catcher Johnny Kling. Besides this battery and their famed infield, the Cubs had Sam (Jimmy) Sheckard stationed in left, Arthur (Circus Solly) Hofman in center, and Frank (Wildfire) Schulte in right.

Altrock drew the White Sox pitching assignment, with Sullivan behind the plate. The great Jiggs Donohue was at first, Isbell at second, Lee Tannehill at short. At third base was an unsung thirty-one-year-old named George Anthony Rohe, an all-time White Sox off his play in this Series. The Sox outfield was Patrick Henry Dougherty in left, Fielder Jones in center, and Edgar Hahn in right.

The historic opener was scoreless until the fifth, with Brown fanning five White Sox in the first three innings. Rohe tripled to lead off the fifth and scored with one out when Kling dropped a throw to the plate. The second and winning White Sox run came in the sixth inning. Jones did the scoring on a hit by Isbell. A sixth-inning wild pitch by Altrock brought in Kling with the Cubs' only run.

With that 2–1 victory behind them, the White Sox had eyes on two in a row as the Series moved to the South Side. Again there were snow flurries. The cold was bitter; attendance suffered. Doc White of the Sox opposed Ed Reulbach on the mound. Jiggs Donohue got the only hit off Reulbach. Dougherty scored the only Sox run as the Cubs won handily,

7–1. Manager Jones had one consolation – the White Sox chose this day to present him with a $500 silver service. Fielder would much rather have had the victory.

Back on the West Side for game number three, it was Walsh vs. Pfiester. Walsh came through with a two-hit shutout, 3–0. Pfiester also pitched creditably, yielding only four hits. His main mistake came in the sixth inning when, with two out and three White Sox on base, he served a high, straight pitch to Rohe. The White Sox third baseman rapped a triple into left field, sending home all three runners.

Altrock and Brown, pitching rivals in the opener, squared off again in the fourth game on the South Side on Columbus Day. Attendance was 18,385, and they enjoyed a pitching treat. Brown pitched a two-hitter (Hahn and Dougherty getting the Sox safeties), and Altrock was nicked for seven blows. Evers singled in Chance with the game's only run, and the 1–0 Cub triumph squared the series at two-all. Gross receipts for the four games were $61,855, with the players to share in $33,401.70.

In the first inning of the fifth game the Cubs scored three times, and the West Side crowd of 23,257 – largest of the Series – scented a rough afternoon for Spitballer Walsh. However he shackled the Cubs with five hits before yielding to Doc White in the seventh. Six White Sox errors contributed to the National Leaguers' scoring, but not enough; the White Sox escaped with an 8–6 decision. They were only one victory from the World Championship.

The Series moved back to the South Side acres. The White Sox chased Brown from the mound with an eight-hit assault in the first one and one-third innings. They then breezed to the title with a final 8–3 triumph. The sixth and deciding game was the only one of the Series captured by a competitor on its home grounds.

Owner Comiskey sweetened the winners' kitty with a $15,000 gift. To him this was a small price to pay for a World

Championship. His Sox had won it; the pennant was flying at Thirty-fifth and Wentworth. The Hitless Wonders had worked a miracle.

Miracles do not happen every day. A long time was to pass before another White Sox manager would duplicate the miracle of '06.

Third place was saved in 1907, the White Sox finishing behind Detroit and the runner-up Athletics. Despite Ed Walsh's 40 victories (against 15 losses) the White Sox could do no better in 1908. The race was a sizzler, and came down to a final-day battle between Detroit and Chicago. Jones named Doc White as Chicago's starter. Detroit knocked out White in the first inning and went on to the championship. Naturally the second-guessers said that Jones should have led off with Frank Smith, the right-handed star boarder in the Chisox doghouse.

Detroit won the pennant with 90 victories and 63 losses. In losing the windup game, Chicago dropped to third (88–64), and Cleveland sneaked into second with 90–64.

Jones had some troubles not of his making that year. The greatest trouble, however, stemmed from his ambition. Comiskey was sincerely fond of the field chief and would have granted any reasonable terms asked by Jones. But when Jones demanded "a partnership or nothing," it was nothing. Jones was through with the big time but for two years (1914–1915) was manager of the St. Louis Federal League team. His successor with the White Sox was little Billy Sullivan, who served only a single campaign.

Today White Sox fans still talk of the 1908 season because of iron-armed Ed Walsh and his 40 victories. Walsh's big 40 forever enshrined his name on the White Sox honor roll.

What kind of a fellow was Ed Walsh? I asked this question of Irving Vaughan, retired *Chicago Tribune* baseball writer, a few months before Walsh's death on May 27, 1959. Vaughan said:

"Walsh was a perfect gentleman, a snappy dresser, and as

powerful as a bull. He was a firm believer in the value of physical fitness, but he seemed to make a hobby of enjoying poor health.

"There never was a pitcher Ed's equal in willingness. He'd make his regular starts and in between serve as a reliever. He actually loved to step in when trouble was on the loose. He made a ceremony of moving from the bull pen to the mound; he was one of those fellows who could strut standing still."

Walsh won only 15 as the White Sox sank to fourth under Sullivan in 1909. He won 18 in 1910, a campaign that marked Hugh Duffy's debut as manager and produced a sixth-place finish. Duffy got them back to fourth in 1911, with Walsh winning 27 victories.

Walsh bagged 27 again in 1912, the year that saw the return of James J. Callahan, who had been skipper in 1903 and part of 1904. Callahan brought Comiskey's men in to fourth in '12, fifth in '13, and sixth in '14, before yielding to Clarence A. (Pants) Rowland in '15. If Callahan's managerial record was a poor one, he did have the satisfaction of seeing the White Sox acquire a legendary battery: Ray (Cracker) Schalk, the little catcher who arrived in 1912, and Urban C. (Red) Faber, a spitballer who checked in in 1914.

The day Schalk reported, he was assigned to catch Doc White against the Athletics and Chief Bender. His story:

"My folks came from Germany. I was born in Harvel, Illinois, where there were only two things to keep a boy busy — playing baseball and cutting weeds on the farm. This may seem like heresy for an old White Sox, but my first idols were the Cubs' Jimmy Archer and Johnny Kling.

"I caught for Litchfield (Illinois) as a youngster. In those days we young'uns played the first games of doubleheaders and imported teams played on the second. One day we had a battery coming from St. Louis — supposed to be hot stuff — and the catcher failed to show. The crowd was impatient and began hollering for young Schalk to catch. That was my start in the big time — at least it looked like big time to me."

Faber once told the *Chicago Tribune*: "When I was eleven years old, my folks staked me to a string ball, a bat, and a glove. I organized one of the two best kid teams in the history of Cascade, Iowa. When I was fourteen I went to Sacred Heart prep school in Prairie du Chien, Wisconsin, and it was there that I began to suspect that a career on the diamond was a good way to avoid a career of milking cows. The idea grew on me when I received two dollars for pitching Sundays for the Dubuque Tigers. And I was certain of my calling when I was raised to five dollars a Sunday at seventeen."

Faber was purchased from Des Moines in 1913, and immediately the White Sox had him pitch against them in the 1913–14 Giants-White Sox world tour. John McGraw, the Giants' Little Napoleon, enjoyed the use of the brilliant young pitcher. A few years later he'd seen entirely too much of him.

CHAPTER 5

Pants Rowland
and Friends

WHITE SOX FANS were introduced to some illustrious newcomers in 1915.

One was Clarence (Pants) Rowland, the "busher from Dubuque" who never in his life played in a major league game. Rowland was to manage the White Sox to another World Championship, in 1917.

Another, better known, was Edward Trowbridge (Cocky) Collins, a hard-hitting twenty-seven-year-old second baseman who already had spent nine years with the Philadelphia Athletics.

Others included Joe Jackson, who had moved over from Cleveland, and Happy Felsch, up from Milwaukee.

Rowland, the son of a railroad engineer, was born in Platteville, Wisconsin, on February 12, 1879. When Clarence was a year old, the Rowlands moved to Dubuque, Iowa, where Charles A. Comiskey had played first base the previous season. While still a grade-schooler, Rowland organized a team known as the Ninth Street Blues. To the *Chicago Tribune*'s Edward Prell, Rowland confessed: "We wore blue blouses, blue caps, and long black stockings borrowed from our sisters. I took a pair of Dad's pants, tucked them under at the knee, and held them in place with a piece of twine."

One day, as Rowland rounded second base, one of the pieces of twine snapped. A pants leg rolled down. Three times he tripped on that pants leg as he sped toward home plate. As he scored, Umpire Billy Baumann said, "Pants, I didn't think you were going to make it." A famous nickname had been born.

Rowland had a varied career before joining the White Sox. He had owned and managed baseball teams in small towns and even been part owner of a café. In 1913 he was owner-manager of the Dubuque club and a White Sox scout when Comiskey asked him to nominate two pitchers who might be added to the Sox squad for the world tour with the Giants. It was on Rowland's advice that Comiskey took Urban (Red) Faber.

In August of 1914, Comiskey was determined to replace Callahan as manager. He invited Rowland in from Peoria, where Pants was managing, on the pretense of talking about Three-I League players. In Chicago, Comiskey told Rowland, "Tell your bosses you won't be back next year. You're going with me."

Rowland had no clew to his job till he again was called to Chicago before the 1914 White Sox-Cubs city series. Comiskey said, "You're not afraid to take my club, are you?"

"No," said Rowland, "and if you think I'm kidding, I'll go down on the field and take charge right now."

The bargain had been struck. Rowland was to lead the White Sox from 1915 through 1918.

Soon after Rowland arrived in his new post he asked Comiskey to obtain Collins from Philadelphia. It was a tall order, for Collins had hit as high as .365 (in 1911) and stolen as many as eighty-one bases in a single season (1910). The cost to Comiskey was fifty thousand dollars.

Collins broke in with the Athletics in 1906. His first major league assignment came on September 18 of that year. It was to pinch-hit against Ed Walsh and the White Sox in Chicago. Collins got the hit!

In 1910, Collins hit safely in all five World Series games

for a .429 average as the Athletics whipped the Chicago Cubs. He held down second base, with Stuffy McInnis at first base, Jack Barry at short, and Frank (Home Run) Baker at third, in the famous Philadelphia "$100,000 infield" that Connie Mack broke up after the 1914 season. Before putting on a White Sox uniform, Collins had played in four World Series for the Athletics.

Collins hit .332 as Rowland's 1915 White Sox moved up to third place. He hit .308 in '16, and the White Sox wound up in second. He hit only .289 in the pennant year of 1917.

The 1917 champions of the American League won 100 games. They never were out of first place after August 18. Happy Felsch, with .308, and Joe Jackson, with .301, led the Chicago hitters. Eddie Cicotte's 28 victories paced the hurling corps.

Players who helped the White Sox qualify for the World Series against John McGraw's Giants included:

Pitchers: Joe Benz, right-hander, six feet one, 194 pounds; Cicotte, right-hander, five feet eight, 160 pounds; David Danforth, left-hander, six feet, 170 pounds; Red Faber, right-hander, six feet, 175 pounds; Ewell (Reb) Russell, left-hander, five feet eleven, 195 pounds; James Scott, right-hander; Claude Williams, left-hander, five feet eleven, 168 pounds; Melvin Wolfgang, right-hander, five feet seven, 160 pounds, mainly used in batting practice.

Catchers: Ray Schalk, five feet eight, 150 pounds; Byrd Lynn, five feet eleven, 170 pounds; Joseph Jenkins, five feet ten, 175 pounds.

Infielders: Edward Collins, five feet nine, 164 pounds; Chick Gandil, six feet two, 196 pounds; Fred McMullin, five feet ten, 165 pounds; Swede Risberg, six feet, 170 pounds; Buck Weaver, five feet eleven, 168 pounds.

Outfielders: John (Shano) Collins, five feet eleven, 175 pounds; Happy Felsch, five feet ten, 175 pounds; Joe Jackson, six feet, 175 pounds; Harry (Nemo) Leibold, five feet five, 154 pounds; Edward Murphy, five feet ten, 160 pounds.

Faber, a 16-game winner during the regular season, de-

feated the Giants three times as the White Sox won the
Series, four games to two. In one game Faber also stole third
base, only to find Weaver already planted on the bag.

Happy Felsch hit a home run as the White Sox won the
opener, 2–1, in Chicago on Saturday, October 6. Cicotte held
the Giants to seven hits.

Chicago won again the next day, 7–2, with Faber handcuffing the Giants on eight hits.

New York's turn came as the World Series moved on to
the Polo Grounds. The Giants' Rube Benton blanked Chicago on five hits, 2–0.

Urban Faber, fine Sox pitcher
of another era.

Chicago was shut out again in the fourth game, 5–0, and the Series was square. New York's Bennie Kauff got the first hit off Faber, the loser, with a home run in the fourth. In the eighth Kauff added another home run off Faber's successor, Danforth.

Back in Chicago Faber went in to relieve in the eighth inning of the fifth game and got credit for the 8–5 triumph. The White Sox, charged with six errors, won on eighth-inning runs by Shano Collins, Eddie Collins, and Joe Jackson.

At the Polo Grounds for the sixth game, Faber started, finished, and won. The score was 4–2, and the White Sox had taken the Series. Joy reigned in Chicago.

The Sox opened the curtailed wartime season of 1918 with the World Championship flag flying. Crepe was hanging by the season's end; the champions mired in sixth place. The 1918 record was 57 victories and 67 losses. Came World Series time, South Side loyalists also had to suffer the indignity of watching the hated Cubs play a World Series in Comiskey Park. It helped that the Cubs lost to the Red Sox, four games to two. Winner of two of those Red Sox victories was George Herman (Babe) Ruth, who was to plague the White Sox for years to come.

Rowland and Comiskey separated. Moved up to command was Coach William (Kid) Gleason, who had been born in Camden, New Jersey, on October 26, 1866. Gleason had enjoyed a long career in the game. He had posted a mark of 129 victories and 129 defeats as a National League pitcher, before putting in fourteen major league seasons as a second baseman.

The Kid's freshman year as manager was a noted one. The White Sox won 88, while losing 52, for a .629 mark and the American League pennant. This, they were saying on the South Side, looked like the greatest of all White Sox teams — perhaps the greatest of all baseball teams. Playing the 1919 World Series against Cincinnati would be only a formality. The White Sox seemed certain to win in a walk.

CHAPTER 6

The White Sox Turn Black

BUT THIS MOST TALENTED of all White Sox teams flopped in the 1919 World Series. They flopped miserably and infamously, and in the process generated more sensational news than any team ever did in winning a World Series. The 1919 World Series will be replayed and reviewed when the 1959 Series is a few small-type lines in the record books.

The White Sox lost the 1919 Series to the Cincinnati Reds, five games to three. On the surface, Cincinnati had pulled off an upset almost as shocking as the four-game shellacking given the Philadelphia Athletics by the Miracle Braves of 1914. Yet even as the 1919 Series was being played, there were scores of baseball folk — from owner Charles A. Comiskey to newspaper reporters — probing below the surface. The evidence they uncovered is basis for the most shocking sports story of all time.

It is the story of the Black Sox.

It is the story of eight Chicago players who allegedly conspired with gamblers and agreed to throw the 1919 Series to the underdog Cincinnati team.

The story is more gruesome because the exact truth never will be known. Those who were betrayed never were able to confirm completely their suspicions and allegations. The betrayers, even if they wished, could not have painted an entirely accurate picture, for there was a maze of plots within the Black Sox plot itself. The double-crossers double-crossed each other, and years later some of them attempted to besmirch noted players by reviving a 1917 incident that was lamentable, but not dishonest. We will always wonder whether one of the accused eight went to his grave an innocent man. We will wonder how well Judge Kenesaw Mountain Landis served justice by expelling the eight from the game after they had been acquitted of a conspiracy by a jury of their peers.

These were the eight whose involvement in the Black Sox conspiracy wrecked one of the greatest baseball teams ever assembled:

Charles Arnold (Chick) Gandil, right-handed-hitting first baseman; born January 19, 1889, in St. Paul, Minnesota. He broke in with the White Sox in 1910, played at Washington and Cleveland before rejoining the White Sox in 1917. He played in 115 games and batted .290 in 1919, his final season. He played in 1,146 major league games and had a lifetime batting average of .276. He was alleged to be one of the ringleaders.

Edward Victor (Knuckles) Cicotte, right-handed pitcher; born June 19, 1884, in Detroit, Michigan. He broke in with Detroit in 1905, played with the Boston Red Sox before moving to Chicago in 1912. He won 28 games in the championship season of 1917; 12 in 1918; 29 in 1919, and 21 in 1920. His lifetime record was 211 victories and 147 losses. He was alleged to be another ringleader.

Joseph Jefferson (Shoeless Joe) Jackson, left-handed-hitting outfielder; born July 16, 1887, in Brandonville, South Carolina; died December 5, 1951. He broke in with Philadelphia in 1908, batted .408 for Cleveland in 1911 but lost bat-

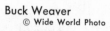
Shoeless Joe Jackson
© Wide World Photo

Buck Weaver
© Wide World Photo

ting title to Ty Cobb's .420. He was traded to the White Sox for $30,000 cash and three players in August, 1915; hit .375 in the 1919 Series; had a lifetime batting average of .356 in 1,330 games. He was one of baseball's superstars.

George Davis (Buck) Weaver, right-handed-hitting third baseman; born August 18, 1890, in Stowe, Pennsylvania; died January 31, 1956, protesting his involvement. He broke in with Chicago in 1912 as shortstop but later shifted to third base. Ty Cobb called him: "The greatest third baseman I ever saw. There was no chance of beating out a bunt on him." Weaver played 1,254 major league games. His lifetime average was .272. Early in his career with the White Sox, he owned a billiard parlor. Later he managed a girls' baseball team in Chicago, and worked in the pari-mutuel department at the race track.

Charles August (Swede) Risberg, right-handed hitting shortstop; born October 13, 1894, in San Francisco. He joined Chicago in 1917, played every infield position in his 476 major league games, all with the White Sox. His lifetime average was .243.

Oscar Emil (Happy) Felsch, right-handed-hitting center fielder; born August 22, 1891, in Milwaukee. He joined the White Sox in 1915, played in 749 major league games and batted .290. The season the Black Sox were exposed, he hit .338.

Claude Preston (Lefty) Williams, southpaw pitcher; born March 9, 1893, in Aurora, Missouri; died in November, 1959, in Laguna Beach, California. He broke in with Detroit in 1913, joined the White Sox in 1916, won 23 games in 1919 and 22 in 1920. His career mark was 81 victories and 45 losses. He was another of the alleged ringleaders.

Frederick William McMullin, utility infielder; born October 13, 1891, in Scammon, Kansas. He joined Chicago in 1916, played in 304 big-league games and averaged .256.

The 1919 Series opened in Cincinnati. The Reds chased Cicotte from the mound in the fourth inning and won, 9–1.

In the second game, the Reds were limited to four hits by Williams but still won, 4–2.

In the first game in Comiskey Park, Dickie Kerr blanked the Reds, 3–0, on three hits. Cincinnati beat Cicotte and the White Sox, 2–0, in the fourth game. A 5–0 shutout over Williams was posted in the fifth game and, as the best five-of-nine series moved back to Cincinnati, the surprising Reds had a four-game-to-one lead.

Chicago took the next two: Kerr won, 5–4, in ten innings, and next day Cicotte, who had asked for the Chicago pitching assignment, baffled the Reds, 4–1.

Back they went to Comiskey Park. Many Chicagoans were now convinced that their heroes had hit their stride and would pull out the Series. But others still suspected funny business. Cincinnati won the Series in the eighth game, routing Williams in the first inning and coasting to a 10–5 victory.

Even before the Series opened, there were rumbles it was rigged for Cincinnati to win. It was, yet many ignored the storm signals out of complete faith in the honesty of the game. For example, when Bob Casey, one of Chicago's most famous reporters, was asked by his office to check on reports that the Series was fixed, he wired back that fixes didn't happen in baseball.

But the shrewd Ring Lardner (one of my predecessors as conductor of the *Chicago Tribune*'s *In the Wake of the News* column) was going about singing "I'm Forever Blowing Ball Games." And the day before the opener, the *Chicago Tribune*'s James Crusinberry had his suspicions aroused. In the lobby of Cincinnati's Sinton Hotel, he saw Abe Attell, the former featherweight champion. Attell was waving a bundle of money and offering to bet on the underdogs from Cincinnati. Crusinberry scouted further; by the third game he had found other signs that something was rotten.

Meanwhile Comiskey was on the scent, but his efforts to investigate were hampered by his team's losses. Some laughed and suggested his suspicions were sour grapes.

Before the fifth game of the Series, Manager Kid Gleason squirmed in the White Sox locker room and said to Harvey T. Woodruff (another predecessor in charge of the *Chicago Tribune's In the Wake of the News*):

"It's the best team that ever went into the World Series. But it isn't playing the baseball that won the pennant for me. I don't know what's the matter, the players don't know what's the matter, but the team has not shown itself thus far."

Following the fifth game, Gleason said to Crusinberry:

"They aren't hitting. . . . The bunch I had fighting in August for the pennant would have trimmed this Cincinnati bunch without a struggle. The bunch I have now couldn't beat a high school team. . . . You know, it doesn't seem possible that this gang that worked so great for me all summer could fall down like this. I tell you, I'm absolutely sick at heart. They haven't played any baseball for me."

After the Reds had won the series, Kid Gleason said, "I tell you, those Reds haven't any business beating a team like the White Sox. We played the worst baseball in all but a couple of games that we have played all year. I don't know yet what was the matter. Something was wrong. I didn't like the betting odds. I wish no one had ever bet a dollar on the team."

But the Series was over and the White Sox had lost. No one had actionable evidence that the fix was in, but Comiskey was so convinced by his investigation that he temporarily held up the pay checks of eight suspects. There were other investigations, official and unofficial, and rumor aplenty, but not much else.

Seven of the eight suspects were back for the 1920 season. Gandil had gotten into a salary dispute with Comiskey and quit the game. Gandil's absence caused a lifting of eyebrows.

Among those still pursuing the investigation was Crusinberry. As he wrote in *Sports Illustrated* (September 17, 1956), he got a break in mid-July while sitting in a New York hotel room with Ring Lardner. Kid Gleason telephoned and said,

"Come up to Dinty Moore's. I'm at the bar with Abe Attell. He's talking, and I want you to hear it."

Lardner and Crusinberry went to Dinty Moore's. They stood at the bar and heard Attell implicate Arnold Rothstein, notorious New York gambler.

Lardner realized how close to the mark he'd been the previous October, and Crusinberry was convinced that he could still blow open the story for the *Chicago Tribune*.

He saw an opening when, in September of 1920, there came a report that a Chicago Cub pitcher had been approached by gamblers to throw a game to the Philadelphia Phillies. A grand jury investigation was demanded. Crusinberry figured that if the grand jury looked into the alleged fixing of a Cub pitcher, it also might be persuaded to examine the 1919 World Series.

So one day the *Chicago Tribune* received a letter signed by

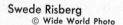

Swede Risberg
© Wide World Photo

Fred M. Loomis, a prominent Chicagoan. Mr. Loomis called attention to rumors about the 1919 Series and pointed out:

> There is a perfectly good grand jury located in this county. The citizens and taxpayers of Illinois are maintaining such an institution for the purpose of investigating any alleged infraction of the law.
>
> Those who possess evidence of any gambling last fall in the World Series should come forward and present it in a manner that may give assurance to the whole country, so that justice will be done in this case where the confidence of the people seems to have been so flagrantly violated.

The grand jury took a cue from the letter. Not until thirty-six years later, in his article in *Sports Illustrated*, did Crusinberry reveal that he had written the letter for Loomis.

Now the betrayers were to be smoked out. Only a few days after publication of the Loomis letter, Assistant State Attorney Hartley L. Replogle said that the grand jury had learned that "The last World Series between the Chicago White Sox and the Cincinnati Reds was not on the square. Five to seven players on the White Sox are involved."

Suddenly attention switched to Philadelphia, where Bill Maharg, a former boxer, had started to talk. Maharg said that he and Bill Burns, a former major league pitcher, had cooked up the conspiracy to involve eight White Sox in throwing the World Series. Perhaps Maharg truly believed that he and Burns, at Burns' instigation, had cooked up the fix. There is other evidence that Burns acted on behalf of another original instigator.

Maharg's statement (as recorded in the *Chicago Tribune*):

> I am a great friend of Bill Burns, the veteran southpaw. After quitting baseball, Burns, who is a Texan, bought oil leases and cleared more than $100,000. In the

middle of September of last year I received a wire from Burns from New York. I hopped a train and met Bill at the Ansonia.

. . . While we were there in the room talking, Eddie Cicotte came in and started to talk in a low voice to Burns. I heard enough to know that he said a group of White Sox players would be willing to throw the coming World Series if a syndicate of gamblers would give them $100,000 on the morning of the first game.

When Cicotte left, Burns turned to me and repeated his conversation, part of which I had heard. Burns said: "Do you know any gamblers who would be interested in this proposition?"

It struck me as a peculiar stunt, and I could hardly believe it. . . . I said I would go back to Philadelphia and see what I could do. Burns said he would have to go to Montreal to close an oil deal and that he would wire me about the progress of the deal.

That explains the telegram Burns sent from Montreal when he wired: "What have you done about ball games?"

I immediately went to Philadelphia and saw some gamblers there. They told me it was a big proposition for them to handle and they recommended me to Arnold Rothstein.

. . . Burns had returned to New York. . . . We met Rothstein by appointment at the Astor and put the proposition up to him. He declined to get into it. He said he did not think such a frame-up could be possible.

. . . I returned to Philadelphia thinking everything was off until I received a telegram from Bill Burns. It read: "Arnold R. has gone through with everything. Got eight in. Leaving for Cincinnati at 4:30."

I went the next day and joined Burns. He said that after I had left New York, he ran into Abe Attell, who made it appear that the matter had been fixed with Rothstein.

Ed Cicotte
© Wide World Photo

Attell was in Cincinnati, quartered in a large suite in the Sinton, and he had a gang of about 25 gamblers with him. He said they were all working for Rothstein, but we learned later that this was fiction — that Rothstein was not in it at all.

Their work was raw. They stood in the lobby of the Sinton and buttonholed everybody who came in. They accepted bets right and left, and it was nothing unusual to see thousand-dollar bills wagered.

I had my first suspicion on the morning of the first game, when Burns and I visited Attell. We asked for the $100,000 to turn over to the White Sox players to carry out our part of the deal.

I want to say right here why the White Sox trusted

Burns. He has the reputation in baseball of always being on the level. His word has always been his bond, and ball players had every confidence in him.

Attell refused to turn over the $100,000, saying they needed the money to make bets. He made a counter-proposition that $20,000 would be handed the players at the end of each losing game. Burns went to the Sox players and they seemed satisfied. . . .

We all bet on Cincinnati the first day and won. The next morning Burns and I went around to Attell again. . . . Stacks of bills were being counted on dressers and tables.

Again Attell stalled us off. . . . We grew suspicious and asked Abe if Rothstein was really in the deal. Then Abe flashed the fake telegram: "Have wired you twenty grand and waived identification. A. R."

. . . We learned later that this was a fake telegram. . . . Burns felt sore because he had no money for the White Sox, and he told me he would turn over $110,000 worth of oil leases to the players as security. I persuaded him not to take this step and thereby saved him that money.

After the second game we raced back to the hotel and again found Attell and his confederates. Attell again made excuses about needing the coin to make further wagers, but did place $10,000 on the table. . . . Burns asked me to take the money and I refused. He finally took it himself and turned it over to one of the players. Burns told me that he saw that the players were restless and wanted the full amount and he was afraid they would not keep up the agreement.

The players, however, told him that if they lost behind Cicotte and Williams they wouldn't win for Kerr, the busher. So we went to Chicago and bet all our personal winnings . . . that Cincinnati would win the third game . . . the Sox got even with us by winning this game.

Burns and I lost every cent we had in our clothes. I had to hock my diamond pin to get back to Philadelphia. The whole upshot of the matter was that Attell and his gang cleaned up, and the Sox players were double-crossed out of $90,000 that was coming to them.

I heard that a new deal was made on the final game . . . but I don't know of that.

The statement by Maharg, who was widely known to baseball players, and a one-time roommate of pitcher Grover Cleveland Alexander, was damaging. Evidence is that Cicotte was first to crack. For a long while he had been under strain and, during the series at Cincinnati, had been seen wandering aimlessly along the streets after the curfew hour.

According to the *Chicago Tribune*, Cicotte went to Comiskey and said, "I don't know what you'll think of me, but I got to tell you how I double-crossed you, Mr. Comiskey. I did double-cross you. I'm a crook. I got $10,000 for being a crook."

"Don't tell it to me," said Comiskey. "Tell it to the grand jury."

When Cicotte told it to the grand jury, he told it with tears in his eyes. He said, "Risberg and Gandil and McMullin were at me for a week before the World Series started. They wanted me to go crooked. . . . I needed the money. I had the wife and the kids. . . .

"I bought a farm. There was a $4,000 mortgage on it. There isn't any mortgage on it now. I paid it off with the crooked money.

"The eight of us — the eight under indictment — got together in my room three or four days before the games started. Gandil was master of ceremonies. We talked about throwing the Series — decided we could get away with it. . . . I told them I had to have the cash in advance. I didn't want any promises.

". . . Then Gandil and McMullin took us all, one by one, away from the others and we talked turkey. They asked me my price. I told them $10,000.

". . . It was Gandil I was talking to. He wanted to give me some money at the time, the rest after the games were played and lost. . . . I stood pat. I wanted that $10,000, and I got it. . . . The day before I went to Cincinnati I put it up to them squarely for the last time that there would be nothing doing unless I had the money.

"That night I found the money under my pillow. There was $10,000. . . . I had been paid, and I went on. I threw the game."

Announcement that the grand jury had indicted the eight Black Sox also prompted Jackson to confess. When Jackson first heard the news, he irately telephoned Judge McDonald and protested that he was an honest man.

"I know you are not," said the judge, slamming down the telephone.

Jackson, in recounting details leading to his confession, said, "I thought it over. I figured somebody had squawked. I got the idea that the place for me was on the ground floor."

Jackson again contacted Judge McDonald and volunteered to give information.

The judge said, "Come on over and tell it to me."

Jackson went and said, "I got $5,000 and they promised me $20,000. All I got was $5,000 that Lefty Williams handed me in a dirty envelope."

A few hours later, Jackson told the *Chicago Tribune*: "A lot of these sporting writers have been roasting me about the third game of the World Series being square. Let me tell you something. The eight of us did our best to kick it and little Dick Kerr won the game by his pitching. Because he won it, these gamblers double-crossed us for double-crossing them. . . . Who gave me the money? Lefty Williams slipped it to me the night before I left for Cincinnati and told me I'd get the other $15,000 after I delivered the goods. . . . Now Risberg threatens to bump me off if I squawk. That's why I had all the bailiffs with me when I left the grand jury room this afternoon."

Legend has it that as Jackson left the grand jury room, a tearful boy pleaded, "Say it isn't so, Joe."

One who believed it was so was Comiskey. Following their appearance before the grand jury, Comiskey notified the accused by telegram:

> You and each of you are hereby notified of your indefinite suspension as a member of the Chicago American League baseball club.
>
> Your suspension is brought about by information which has just come to me directly involving each of you in the baseball scandal now being investigated by the present grand jury of Cook County resulting from the World Series of 1919.
>
> If you are innocent of all wrong doing, you and each of you will be reinstated; if you are guilty, you will be retired from organized baseball for the rest of your lives if I can accomplish it.
>
> Until there is a finality to this investigation, it is due to the public that I take this action, even though it cost Chicago the pennant.

Comiskey's action was decisive. Whether it cost Chicago the pennant is doubtful. When the stars were banned, the White Sox still had a chance to head off the Cleveland Indians for the American League championship, but only a slim chance.

At the conclusion of the regular season, and before Cleveland defeated the Brooklyn Dodgers, five games to two, in the World Series, Comiskey called in his players. To ten who had been beyond reproach in the scandal, he gave checks for $1,500 each. Immediately the ten issued this statement:

To the Fans of Chicago:

We, the undersigned players of the Chicago White Sox, want the world to know the generosity of our employer who, of his own free will, has reimbursed each and every member of our team the difference between the winning and losing share of last year's World Series, amounting to approximately $1,500.

The statement was signed by Schalk, Faber, Eddie and John Collins, Leibold, Kerr, Murphy, Wilkinson, McClellan, and Lynn. And each and every one of them believed that if the great Faber had been healthy enough to pitch in the 1919 Series, the greatest of all White Sox teams would have beaten Cincinnati, fix or no.

The scandal did not end with the indictment of the eight Black Sox. It took some while to bring the miscreants to trial; then they refused to testify against themselves; Abe Attell, a key witness, refused to identify himself as the Abe Attell mentioned in the testimony; and much of the grand jury testimony was lost. Finally the eight were exonerated.

But Judge Kenesaw Mountain Landis, baseball's new commissioner, acted on his own. He issued an edict that forever banned the eight from performing in the major leagues. His decision was weakly contested, but it stuck.

The Black Sox scandal did not die out. Perhaps it never will. A few years later Swede Risberg popped back into the news, declaring that in 1917 there had been fixed games that permitted the White Sox to win the pennant leading to their glorious World Championship. Early in January of 1927, Risberg came to Chicago to testify before Judge Landis that the White Sox had paid between $1,000 and $1,100 to the Detroit Tigers for throwing four games late in the 1917 race. He implicated Manager Clarence (Pants) Rowland, Red Faber, and Eddie Collins, among others. His charges were corroborated by Gandil, then coaching a company baseball team at the copper mines in Hurley, New Mexico.

Actually, the Risberg allegations were nothing new. He merely gave a different impression of a known fact of the 1917 season: that the White Sox players had taken up a special purse for some of the Detroit Tigers.

Risberg alleged that the purse had been collected to pay off the Tigers for blowing four games (two doubleheaders) to the White Sox during the closing stages of a tight pennant race. It was alleged that all of the White Sox, except Manager Rowland and Weaver, contributed to the purse. Another allegation was that Eddie Collins said as he paid his $45 assessment to Gandil, "I don't like this — I'll never do it again."

Most of the White Sox agreed that a special purse had been contributed to the Tigers. They said, however, that Risberg's charges were false — that the money had not been paid to the Tigers for losing the two doubleheaders, which the Tigers had done, but in appreciation of the Tigers' winning three in a row from Boston during a later stage of the race.

Testimony was that before the crucial set of Chicago-Detroit doubleheaders, a Detroit player had approached Gandil under the Comiskey Park seats and said, "These are going to be some pretty soft games."

Then, allegedly, Gandil had answered, "Well, if it goes all right I will see that you are fixed up for it."

According to the story, Gandil called Detroit's Bill James out of a poker game and said, "Here's a little donation from our boys."

The money was paid. Gandil, Risberg, and even Felsch later suggested it was a payoff. The others involved said it was a token of appreciation for Detroit's success against Boston. Testimony of some of the game's most brilliant stars indicated that the White Sox players, though perhaps guilty of an error in judgment, had acted in good faith. Risberg's charges quickly fell by the wayside.

As time passed, there was continuing conjecture about the Black Sox scandal. Sentiment was that some — particularly Weaver — had been harshly treated. The contradictions and discrepancies in the case led a few to believe that if the entire story could be told it might vindicate one or more of the banished players.

Then, in 1956, Gandil told his story in *Sports Illustrated*. He had some new twists. He said that he had been approached in Boston about a week before the 1919 World Series by J. J. (Sport) Sullivan, a long-time acquaintance. He said that Sullivan suggested to him and Cicotte that perhaps seven or eight White Sox players might be interested in throwing the World Series to Cincinnati.

Gandil said he told Sullivan the plot could not work, whereupon Sullivan said, "Don't be silly. It's been pulled before and it can be again."

According to Gandil, Sullivan was willing to pay $10,000 to each of the miscreants. Then, Gandil admitted, he and Cicotte agreed to take in Jackson, Weaver, Risberg, Felsch, McMullin, and Williams. They met one night, Gandil went on, and Weaver suggested that they be paid in advance. It was Weaver's idea, said Gandil, that if the plot became too hot, the White Sox could double-cross Sullivan and not only keep the fixers' money but collect the winners' share of the Series purse.

Gandil's *Sports Illustrated* article said that he then had a meeting with Sullivan, who told him it would take some time to raise the cash for the players. Later, as the season closed, according to Gandil, Cicotte introduced him to Bill Burns, the former pitcher. Burns asked that the White Sox do nothing about Sullivan's overture until Burns could contact a friend.

Gandil wrote that then he and Cicotte called a meeting and told of Burns' offer. Weaver suggested, "We might as well take his money, too, and go to hell with all of them." This contradicted Weaver's plea that he was an innocent victim who had rebuffed the fixers.

Gandil wrote that Sullivan brought a friend to meet him in the Warner Hotel in Chicago, that he recognized the friend as Arnold Rothstein, and that Rothstein suggested the White

Sox try their best to win the first game, thus making Chicago a prohibitive favorite to take the Series. But when the White Sox wanted $80,000 in advance, Rothstein balked. "What's to assure us you guys will keep the agreement?"

Gandil said in his story that the players would give their word. Rothstein's reported response: "It's a weak collateral."

Finally, said Gandil, Rothstein compromised. He would pay $10,000 in advance, and the remaining $70,000 in installments. When the players agreed, Rothstein put up $10,000 in $1,000 bills. The players decided to slip the money to Cicotte. It was their thought that Cicotte would keep the money until it could be changed inconspicuously. Cicotte put the money under his pillow.

Now, Gandil went on, Rothstein insisted they be quiet about the plot. The players agreed, and also decided to take whatever money might be obtained from Burns.

He said that in Cincinnati he and Cicotte were visited by Burns and Attell. Attell allegedly produced a telegram that said: WILL TAKE YOU IN ON ANY DEAL YOU MAKE. WILL GUARANTEE ALL EXPENSES. A. R.

According to Gandil, the players were nonplused because they knew of their private deal with Rothstein. Gandil said that later, when the players had misgivings, Sullivan warned: "I wouldn't call it the best policy to double-cross Rothstein."

After the first game, Gandil said, no one showed up to pay the White Sox the next payment on their $70,000. He hinted that Cincinnati's second-game victory was legitimate.

Then, after Chicago won the third game, Gandil claimed he was visited by Burns, and that Burns was panicked. Burns said that some gamblers, believing the Series was fixed, had bet on the Reds and lost because of Kerr's victory. Gandil said that since he had little faith in Burns, he wouldn't consider Burns' offer of $20,000 for assuring continuation of the fix.

Gandil went on to tell how he drove in Weaver with the winning run in the tenth inning of the sixth game. The White

Sox won the seventh game, too, and Gandil testified that every man was honestly attempting to pull out the Series.

No one will ever know. All that shows in the record books is that the White Sox lost the World Series of 1919 and finished second in the 1920 pennant race; and that eight of the 1919 team were banished from baseball for life.

They were the Black Sox. Some were blacker than others, but they all suffered. Baseball never went after the fixers.

The White Sox were ruined. Few realized how great the ruin could be. It would be another forty years before Chicago again won an American League pennant.

CHAPTER 7

Picking Up the Pieces

Now IT WAS 1921, and time for baseball to begin picking up the pieces left by the Black Sox bombshell.

As a whole, the sport rebounded spectacularly, thanks to a bushy-browed headliner named Judge Kenesaw Mountain Landis and a spindly-legged power hitter named George Herman (Babe) Ruth. In January, at a meeting in Chicago, the sixteen major league clubs officially designated Landis as commissioner and gave him a rich seven-year contract. In the ensuing months, Babe Ruth was to smash out a record 59 home runs, changing perhaps forever the pattern of the game. From this point on, there would be increased demand for players able to drive a baseball out of the park, and the thrill of the home run would help fans forget their betrayal by the Black Sox.

But if a new era had dawned, it would be a long time before the White Sox and their loyalists saw the sunrise. Thirty-five seasons of frustration and despair would pass before the Chicago South Siders, in Al Lopez's freshman year as skipper, again finished as high as second place.

Kid Gleason, his heart as heavy as the Old Roman's after the Black Sox exposé, was rehired as manager in January of

1921, a few weeks before Leslie M. O'Connor — destined to be White Sox general manager many years later —was introduced to baseball as secretary to Commissioner Landis.

Gleason's 1921 White Sox won only 62 games and tumbled to seventh. Next season they were fifth with a 77–77 record. But when they toppled back to seventh, with only 69 victories, in 1923, the gray-haired Kid decided he was finished. As soon as the '23 White Sox closed out a city series triumph over the Cubs, Gleason assembled his players and told them they would be working for a new pilot in '24. Some of the White Sox cried openly.

Then, after the *Chicago Tribune* had printed an exclusive revealing Gleason's plans, the Kid went to Comiskey's office and formally resigned.

Comiskey pleaded, but Gleason was firm, his mind set. The eyes of both men were misty at the final handshake.

Gleason returned to his home in Philadelphia. For a long while he barely ate, and refused to see friends. He was near total collapse, and those who knew him were gravely concerned. At the 1924 World Series he was offered a coaching job by Connie Mack, but not until the following spring did he accept it. Nine years later, still grieving the past, Gleason died in Philadelphia. Mack said softly, "He never once failed me in the slightest way. We are going to miss him more than I can tell."

By the first Saturday of the '21 season, after dropping a 7–5 decision to Ty Cobb's Tigers, the White Sox were in fourth place. For the rest of the season they floundered around in the second division, saving just a little face by beating the Cubs five in a row in the October city series.

Meanwhile, Babe Ruth's home run bat was pacing the Yankees to their first American League flag. Five of Ruth's homers were at the expense of Chicago hurlers; Dickie Kerr and lefty John Wienecke gave up two each, Red Faber one. Faber won 25 games and lost 15, posting a 2.48 earned-run mark. The veteran Eddie Collins topped Chicago's hitters

Johnny Evers managed the Pale Hose in 1924.

Eddie Collins, the classiest Sox of them all.

with .337, while Early Sheely, the rookie first baseman, drove in 95 runs and hit 11 homers. Harry Hooper, the long-time Red Sox outfielder, joined the club at the age of thirty-three and batted .327. 1921 marked the first full season's play for Bib August Falk, who had come up from the University of Texas, and John Anthony Mostil, a ball-hawking center fielder. Falk played through 1928, then went to Cleveland, Mostil stayed on until 1929.

Mostil, later to become the chief White Sox scout, was reared within a few blocks of both the old and present parks. His introduction to the Old Roman came in 1907: Young Johnny, caught attempting to slip into the old park on Thirty-fifth Street, and nipped by the club's police dog, was hauled before Comiskey for a dressing down.

On the night of July 4, 1918, Johnny — then a semi-pro in the Whiting, Indiana, area — received a telephone call from Harry Grabiner, who had heard of him through a cab driver. At Grabiner's insistence, Mostil reported the next day and got a few drives off Joe Benz in batting practice. Manager Pants Rowland let him sit on the bench that afternoon, and when Buck Weaver was hurt sliding into third, he scored the game's winning run as a pinch runner.

Mostil played ten games at second base through the rest of the season, at a $150 per month salary. During spring training of 1919, at Mineral Wells, Texas, he was working out at second and was nearly decapitated by a Joe Jackson liner. Immediately he was sent to the outfield by Manager Gleason and subsequently optioned to Milwaukee. In 1921 he reapppeared, and by the season's end he was a full-fledged regular.

Total attendance for the '21 city series was 76,788. Kerr gave up only five hits as the White Sox defeated Grover Alexander and the Cubs, 2–0, in the opener. Faber and Buzz McWeeney shared the White Sox pitching assignment in the 8–5 second-game victory. The White Sox then reeled off 4–3, 3–2, and 9–5 wins.

1922, a year marked by the death of Adrian C. (Cap) Anson, star of the long-ago White Stockings who had inspired
the name for Comiskey's White Sox, began with the almost
unanimous selection of the White Sox to finish in last place.
The fate seemed sealed when Dick Kerr, a 19-game winner
in '21, was suspended after his long holdout. Kerr's absence
was to be felt for more than one season, too, because he did
not put on a Chicago uniform again until 1925.

The '22 White Sox *were* in the basement late in May, but
they rallied and lost fourth place only on the last day of the
season. The year saw Collins (.337) again topping the hitters
and Faber winning 21 and losing 17. Catcher Ray Schalk hit
a single, double, triple, and homer in a June 27 game with
Detroit.

At the close of the regular campaign, the White Sox invaded the Cubs' park to win the city series opener, 6–2, the
thirteenth consecutive victory over their National League
rivals! The streak ended the following day with a 10–3 Cub
win in White Sox Park. Oscar Grimes' three-run homer beat
the Sox, 8–5, in the third game, and the series was even when
Dixie Leverett bested Grover Alexander, 1–0, on Sheely's
grounder.

With a five-run sixth-inning assault on Ted Blankenship,
an 8–10 pitcher during the regular season, the Cubs took the
fifth game, 7–2. Red Faber hooked up with Tiny Osborne,
already winner of two in the series, in the sixth game. Faber
yielded three hits, Osborne four. The Sox won, 1–0, as Schalk
bunted home Sheely in the ninth. Next day, Alexander
blanked the Sox, 2–0. The Old Roman's White Sox had lost
their first city series since 1909.

But despite all their disappointments, the Sox had been the
main party to the most sensational contest of 1922 — the 2–0
perfect game that their right-hander Charles Culbertson
Robertson had flung at the Tigers on April 30.

Robertson had appeared in only one major league game
when he joined the club in '22. In his first full year, he won

14 and lost 15, and pitched the first perfect game since Boston's Ernie Shore bested Washington, 4–0, on June 23, 1917, and the last until Yankee Don Larsen's masterpiece against the Dodgers in 1956.

Robertson was born January 31, 1897, in Sherman, Texas. He graduated from Austin College and was playing with the Sherman team when the Sox bought him for $250 down, plus $1,750 if he made good. After his tour of duty with the air service, his single appearance with Chicago in 1919, and his time with Minneapolis, Robertson was recalled in 1922. Commissioner Landis advised the White Sox to give the Sherman team its remaining $1,750.

The April 30 game took place in Detroit's Navin Field. Attendance was estimated at 25,000, and some fans overflowed onto the field. Only seven of Robertson's pitches were hit on the ground. Shortstop Eddie Mulligan did not have a fielding chance.

Chicago got to Detroit pitcher Herman Pillette for a pair of runs in the second inning. After four futile innings against Robertson, some of the Tigers began thinking that the Chicago pitcher might be tampering with the ball. Detroit outfielder Harry Heilmann called for Umpire Dick Nallin to inspect the ball. The umpire could find no evidence of trickery. Subsequently the Tigers inspected first baseman Sheely's glove, and Manager Ty Cobb even frisked Robertson. The fiery Cobb years later wrote the *Chicago Tribune*'s Irving Vaughan: "As to Robertson, I hope you don't think that a man at the plate doesn't know when a pitcher is sailing a ball or throwing a ball with a black smudge on it. Robertson didn't have outstanding pitching ability."

Following Robertson's game, Detroit President Frank Navin admitted skepticism but added, "The Detroit club, however, is unwilling to cast any reflection on Robertson's pitching or detract in any way from his performance."

The only threat to Robertson's perfect game had come in the second: Mostil had to race toward the crowd in deep left to haul down a strong drive by Bobby Veach. It was the first and last time Mostil played left. Mostil also made the final put-out, dragging down a pinch fly by Johnny Bassler and falling into the crowd. The ball was wrested from him.

As Mostil came in without the ball, Manager Gleason said, "You'd better grab a ball and tell Charley it was the one you caught." All the White Sox autographed a discard for the unsuspecting perfect game hero.

Robertson won 13 games for the White Sox in 1923, but never more than eight in any season thereafter. He pitched for the Browns in 1926, and wound up his career in '27 and '28 with the Boston National League club. His lifetime victory total was 49, including the BIG one.

In 1923 few of the White Sox saw any chance of heading off New York's bid for a third consecutive American League championship. And a dismal season it was, winding up with Manager Gleason's resignation. Still, the White Sox introduced some interesting players: Willie Kamm, the twenty-three-year-old third baseman obtained for $100,000 from San Francisco; pitcher Hollis (Sloppy) Thurston, who won 7 and lost 8 after being obtained from St. Louis; and left-hander Michael John Cvengros, a twenty-one-year-old who was not to do much after winning 12 in his first season with the Sox.

Again Red Faber proved the most dependable pitcher, winning 14 and losing 11. Again Collins topped the hitters, this time with a mark of .360, but failed to win the batting crown. Harry Heilmann got it with .403. Babe Ruth, with .393, Tris Speaker, with .380, and George (the Bull) Uhle, with .361, also topped Collins.

Though no artistic success, the 1923 season was a memorable one in White Sox history for the discovery of Theodore Amer Lyons, a right-hander born December 28, 1900, in Lake Charles, Louisiana. Ted may have been the greatest pitcher ever to appear in the American League, considering his performances came during the years of the White Sox famine. He was to win 260 games before calling it a career.

Lyons was an infielder when he enrolled at Baylor University in Waco, Texas, in 1920. There he saw an overabundance of infielders and switched to pitching. As a freshman, Lyons won ten games, and the Philadelphia Athletics came after him. Lyons, ambitious to study law, sparred with the Athletics over their offer to pay his way through college. He continued to spar with all interested until, with a record of 27 victories and 8 losses, he began his senior year. Then White Sox catcher Ray Schalk, tipped off by the Baylor coach, dropped in from the Chicago training camp in Waco.

Schalk, who had caught Robertson's perfect game, knew a pitcher when he saw one. The Cracker sent a wire to Harry Grabiner in Chicago with advice to sign Lyons quickly. The White Sox finally got Ted's name on a $300-a-month contract. Lyons caught up with the White Sox in St. Louis early in July. With Gleason ill, substitute manager Collins sent in Lyons as a relief pitcher. Ted's head was in the clouds.

Lyons won two games and lost one in '23, and saw limited action in a pair of city series games. The White Sox, after losing the first two (8–4 and 4–3) rallied to win back the Chicago championship with 4–2, 5–3, 7–4, and 4–3 victories before a total crowd of 141,791.

Gleason's resignation left fans pondering on his successor. A few thought of Collins, but it wasn't Eddie's turn.

Late in October, Comiskey announced the appointment of Frank Leroy Chance, forty-six, the Peerless Leader of Tinker-to-Evers-to-Chance fame, who after a long stretch managing the Cubs managed the Red Sox in '23.

Illness soon hit the Peerless Leader. On February 17, 1924, he wired his resignation to Comiskey. The Old Roman declined to accept it. He declared Chance could take over the managerial duties when he was recovered; meanwhile the job was entrusted to Johnny Evers, Chance's former Cub teammate, an erstwhile Cub pilot, and currently a White Sox coach. Chance did get to Chicago in April, immediately was hospitalized, and then returned to his California home for recuperation. He died in September.

Under the forty-one-year-old Evers, who had been in charge since spring training in Winter Haven, Florida, the White Sox wound up last with a mark of 66 won, 87 lost. Boston was seventh with 67 won and 87 lost; Cleveland finished sixth with 67 won, 86 lost. As late as their final series with Boston, the Sox could have captured sixth.

As usual they won the city series, this time four games to two.

Collins' batting average slipped to .349, and Bib Falk beat him out of the team batting title with .352. Harry Hooper hit ten homers for the second year in a row. Sloppy Thurston pitched twenty victories; Faber fell to nine.

Comiskey had some sympathy for Evers' poor showing: Evers himself had been ailing; the White Sox had lost their regular shortstop, Harvey McClellan, for all but thirty-two games, and catcher Schalk was beginning to show signs of wear. Yet the Old Roman felt the time had come for Eddie Collins to take over as manager.

Appointment of Collins, then thirty-seven, was announced on December 11. Comiskey said, "Collins has been popular with our patrons ever since he has been with the team. I think he has earned the right to become manager."

Evers temporarily retired from baseball, later served with the Boston Braves organization. After a long period of failing health, he died in Albany, New York, on March 28, 1947.

No one can accuse fortune of smiling on Eddie Collins in his first term as manager; yet Chicago finished fifth (79–75) after a ding-dong battle with St. Louis (82–71) and Detroit (81–73). Collins, his .346 leading the hitting, suffered a leg infection late in August, and the White Sox struggled on without his second base play. Harry Hooper was temporarily sidelined with a blood clot. An ailment diagnosed as gallstones prevented the return to the line-up of McClellan. Maurice Archdeacon, the fleet outfielder, was handicapped by tonsilitis, and finally released. The club also gave up on pitcher Cvengros as Collins made an almost wholesale shuffling of his personnel. On the bright side, catcher Ray Schalk returned to pre-1924 form behind the plate.

Ted Lyons had his first great pitching year, winning 21, including a one-hitter against Washington on September 19. (The spoiler was Bobby Veach, who punched out a ninth-inning hit.) Ted Blankenship won 17 while losing 8. Red Faber won 12. Johnny Mostil led the league in stolen bases, and Sheely batted in 111 runs.

This time the city series was a different story. The Cubs, after finishing last for the first time in history, rose up and smote their cross-town tormentors.

The first game, played in Comiskey Park on October 7, was one of the most noted of the long rivalry. For nineteen innings, the Cubs' Grover Alexander and the White Sox cowboy, Ted Blankenship, dueled on the mound. The score was 2–2 when darkness set in.

Lyons and Dickie Kerr, who returned from exile in '25, pitched for the White Sox in the second game. The Cubs won, 2–1, and won the next game, 8–2. After Blankenship had won, 7–2, the Cubs closed it out with 3–1 and 7–4 victories.

Shortstop Harvey McClellan, not quite twenty-nine, died of cancer on November 16, 1925.

Lyons won 18, including a 6–0 no-hitter at Boston on August 21, as the White Sox retained fifth (81–72) in 1926. Faber had a 15–8 mark. Falk hit .345 and Collins .344. It took seven games to beat the Cubs in the city series, the White Sox winning the second, 10–5, the fourth, 4–0, the fifth, 3–1, and the seventh, 3–0.

On November 11, owner Comiskey announced that waivers were being asked on Collins, one of the greatest of all-time Sox heroes, and that the reins were being turned over to Ray Schalk, the scrappy little war horse. In Philadelphia, Collins said he was "surprised." He hooked up again with Connie Mack and batted .338 for the A's in 1927.

CHAPTER 8

From Schalk to Onslow

No one could ever call Charles A. (the Old Roman) Comiskey less than shrewd in his business. When it came time to replace the popular Collins, Comiskey tabbed another White Sox immortal who would be accepted readily by South Side partisans. The new manager was Cracker Schalk, of course — as fine a fellow as ever drew on the White Sox flannels.

In 1927, Schalk brought the club in fifth, a commendable feat for a new manager dealing with athletes who had known him as a player and friend. Lyons won 22 and Al Thomas, the young right-hander, bagged 19. Falk had a .327 season at the plate.

The season of 1928 was memorable if not conspicuously successful. It marked the first appearance in White Sox uniform of Edward Arthur Walsh, son of Big Edward Augustin Walsh, shortstop Billy Cissell, Arthur (the Great) Shires. The season of 1928 also marked Cracker Schalk's exit from the team he had served so long, and so well.

Announcement of Schalk's resignation came after a July 4 doubleheader. Schalk admitted Comiskey had asked for the resignation. Many felt, and Schalk always felt, that he should have been permitted to finish the season.

Ray Schalk, tiny but king-sized in talent.

Now the toga fell to Coach Russell (Lena) Blackburne, born October 23, 1886. Blackburne had been an infielder in 1909 when Comiskey got him from the Providence team for Jakey Atz, Mike Welday, and $8,500. But Lena twisted a knee in spring training at Waco in 1910 and, though he played in 520 major league games, 320 of them for the Sox, he never fully recovered.

The 1928 White Sox, who at Schalk's dismissal were just beginning to recover from a shaky start, settled down to salvage fifth place again. They lost the city series, four games to three. Al Thomas won 17 games, Lyons 15, and Faber 13. Young Walsh won 4 and lost 7. Willie Kamm's .308 topped the hitters.

Clearly, Manager Blackburne had not worked miracles. Nor would he, in his next and last season as a big-league manager. But even as a seventh-place finisher he'd never be forgotten. The Great Shires would see to that!

Purchased from Waco, Arthur Shires was barely twenty-one when he reported to the White Sox in Boston in 1928. The big, boastful first baseman blasted a triple and three singles in his first major league game and batted .341 in 33 freshman contests. In the spring of 1929 he was assigned to the regular first base post and, unbelievably, the team captaincy. The captain's post was taken away from him before the White Sox left Texas, and he was suspended for breaking training.

Came his reinstatement, and on May 15 Whataman took batting practice in a blazing-red hat. Manager Blackburne fined him $100 and suspended him again; but after that day's game against Boston, Shires was back in the clubhouse. Fists flew. In a minute, Blackburne had a black eye, and Shires was at his locker packing his equipment, starting to cry. It appeared that Whataman Shires' brief and glorious career was ending. But it had barely begun.

After Blackburne's announcement that Shires was out, the big fellow was reinstated again. Then came the red-letter night of September 14, 1929, in a Philadelphia hotel.

Blackburne heard sounds of merriment coming from the room of Shires and Douglas Taitt. He investigated and found Shires lifting the cup that cheers. A rematch of the clubhouse fight started and Taitt rushed to get Lou Barbour, the club's traveling secretary.

One report had it that Shires warned Barbour, "Stay out of this! I can lick a dozen like you."

Others said that Shires drove Blackburne and Barbour under

the bed. The gendarmes were summoned, and when Whataman was finally led away Blackburne had two black eyes and
Barbour a badly bitten finger. First Blackburne and then Shires
were accused of biting that finger; but finally, as time made
it the hero of the affair, the view gained currency that Barbour himself had bitten it while the three were grappling. In
1957, Barbour told that it wasn't true, that one of the others
had done the foul deed.

Not even the Philadelphia brawl was the end for Shires.
With the baseball season over and Blackburne gone, there was
little to restrain him in the winter of 1929–30. He decided he
would resume his prize-fighting career and found encouragement from Promoter James C. Mullen, a colorful Chicagoan.
On December 9, the Great Shires needed only twenty-one
seconds to flatten Mysterious Dan Daly in Chicago's tiny
White City arena. For the moment, he was a hero, but sub-
sequent developments indicated the outcome had been assured
in advance.

Now Shires, 189 pounds, was matched with George Trafton, 219-pound Chicago Bears' football center. Over 5,000
jammed their way into White City for the December 16
battle. Shires was down three times in the first round. Wearied
by the feverish pace, both fighters wandered aimlessly through
four more rounds. Trafton gained the decision.

The defeat did not dampen Shires' ambition. Nor did the
revelation that Mysterious Dan Daly had been a coached
teen-ager from Columbus, Ohio. On December 26, Shires
disposed of Bad Bill Bailey in Buffalo in eighty-two seconds.
On January 7, 1930, in St. Paul, Minnesota, a former American Association pitcher named Tony Faeth lasted but two
minutes before "the Idol of Baseball." Al Spohrer, a bald Boston Braves' catcher, succumbed on a four-round technical
knockout in Boston on January 10.

Meanwhile, the offers were pouring in; Whataman was a
gate attraction if nothing else. From Peoria, 150-pound Chief
Coy, who proclaimed himself "the superathlete of the age,"

asked for a fight and declared, "After I beat Shires, I will answer any question on the Bible, history, or literature, for twenty-five minutes." An Illinois horseshoer added another challenge.

But Shires was not interested in Chief Coy or the horse-shoer; he had his sights set on a match with the Chicago Cubs' great hitting star, Hack Wilson. Hack was interested despite objections of his employers. He had fought for nothing — in-formally, of course — so Promoter Mullen's $10,000–$15,000 guarantee was irresistible.

But on January 18, Commissioner Landis summoned the Great Shires for a chat. The judge spoke softly but showed a big stick. After the session Shires declared he was retiring as a fighter. Landis issued a statement: "Hereafter any person connected with any club in this organization who engages in professional boxing will be regarded by this office as having permanently retired from baseball."

So Shires turned to wage negotiations for the 1930 season. At his Texas home he was asked by a reporter, "Are you and Mr. Comiskey close on salary?"

"I'm sure we'll be able to get together," said Whataman.

"How much are you asking?"

"Twenty-five thousand."

"How much has Mr. Comiskey offered?"

"Six thousand."

Shires and Comiskey did get together, but in June, just be-fore the trading deadline, they parted ways permanently. The Great One was sent to Washington for pitcher Garland Braxton and catcher Bennett Tate. Whataman joined Wash-ington in rare form. He visited Congress and told the Repre-sentatives that they were "just a big bunch of plow hands like we are, and used to have a ragged seat in their pants."

He announced to Al Schacht: "I understand you're a pretty well-dressed fellow. Well, when you see me, hide." Schacht was not surprised; he had heard Paul Richards tell how Shires, when he visited Waxahachie in his first season with the White

Sox, had changed his outfit five times in one afternoon just to stroll around town.

And at Washington Shires had the final say about Blackburne: "Gin is not good for an athlete. Walter Johnson told me so. Lena Blackburne didn't tell me so. He just told me I couldn't drink it. He didn't appeal to my reason."

Shires played in thirty-eight games with Washington that season, went back to the minors, and closed out his big-league career with the Braves in 1932.

Late in September of 1929, after his dismissal at Pittsburgh, Donie Bush was summoned to Chicago from his Indianapolis home. Over dinner at the Edgewater Beach Hotel, Bush received the offer to replace Blackburne. It came from Harry Grabiner, the general manager, and Ernest S. Barnard, the American League president, who was keeping an eye on White Sox affairs for the ailing Old Roman. Bush accepted the offer and went home to Indianapolis to await the formal signing. On his arrival he learned that Ed Barrow of the New York Yankees had been phoning him frantically.

Bush returned Barrow's call. The Yankee front office chief told him that Miller Huggins probably couldn't live another day, and Colonel Ruppert wanted him to manage the Yankees.

Donie was stunned. Finally he said, "I've just agreed to manage the White Sox. I gave my word. But if you can get me released from the agreement, I'll come."

The Yankees telephoned Barnard. Barnard telephoned Bush and pleaded, "You're the man the White Sox need."

"I agreed to the White Sox terms," said Bush.

Bush made his word his bond, at a great price.

Carl Reynolds hit .359 for Bush's seventh-place 1930 White Sox, but the league batting title went to the Athletics' Al Simmons (.381). The season introduced two important newcomers to White Sox fans: Lucius Benjamin (Luke) Appling, a twenty-two-year-old shortstop who played in six games and batted .308; Smead Powell Jolley, a slugging twenty-eight-year-old outfielder who played 152 games and hit .313. Appling was to play more games at shortstop (2,218) than any other man in baseball history; make Comiskey Park resound with the chant "C'mon, Luke"; and, with .388 in 1936 and .328 in 1943, give the White Sox their only American League individual batting championships. Jolley Boosters, whose boosters were even better organized, was to prove at an inopportune moment that it was possible to make three errors while playing one fly ball.

The White Sox found Appling with Atlanta of the Southern Association. They announced his purchase — for $25,000 — the same day they signed Raymond Allen (Rip) Radcliff, a first baseman who was to take longer coming up.

Appling got to Chicago at the tag end of the regular season and stayed to see the White Sox lose to Roger Hornsby's Cubs in the city series, four games to two.

Manager Donie Bush began singing Appling's praises soon after the White Sox reported in San Antonio for 1931 spring training. In the regular season Luke played in 96 games and hit .232. The veteran Lu Blue, acquired from the St. Louis Browns, hit .304 as a first baseman. Lew Fonseca, obtained from Cleveland for Willie Kamm, hit .312. Vic Frasier, a rookie right-hander, was the top pitcher with 13 wins, and never won so many again. Faber and Cecil Caraway won 10 each. Lyons slipped to 4 victories.

And the White Sox, with only 56 triumphs, fell into the cellar for the first time since 1924. Still they took the city series, winning the first (9–0), fourth (4–3), fifth (13–6), and seventh, (7–2).

At season's end Fonseca received a summons from Harry Grabiner, who said that Comiskey wanted him to replace Bush. On October 26, only two weeks after Fonseca's signing, the Old Roman died. His passing, preceded earlier in the year by the death of President Ernest Sargent Barnard and Byron Bancroft Johnson, the retired president, left Connie Mack and Clark Griffith as the American League patriarchs.

It also left the White Sox in charge of the Old Roman's son, J. Louis Comiskey.

Nor was the 1932 debut of J. Louis and Manager Lew an auspicious one. The White Sox lost 102 games, a club record, and saved seventh place only because the Red Sox dropped 111. Meanwhile, the cross-town Cubs were latching onto another pennant.

Smead Jolley was shipped off to Boston. Suitcase Bob Seeds, after batting .000 in a pair of games for Cleveland, joined the White Sox and hit .291 to lead the batters. The only other highlight was a Memorial Day free-for-all with veteran umpire George Moriarty. American League President Will Harridge slapped $500 fines on pitcher Milt Gaston, reportedly knocked down three times by Moriarty, and Fonseca, who said he struck no blows. Catcher Charley Berry, later to become a major league umpire, was fined $250; catcher Frank Grube's levy was $100. Umpire Moriarty was severely reprimanded.

In planning for 1933, Fonseca and Lou Comiskey realized the White Sox would have to take stern measures to avoid a repetition of the disaster of 1932. Then they learned that Connie Mack was about to break up the Athletic team that had won the 1929, 1930, and 1931 pennants.

Comiskey gave Mack $150,000 for Jimmy Dykes, Mule Haas, and Al Simmons. In another transaction, pitcher George Earnshaw, who had won 24, 22, 21, and 19 in the past four seasons, came to Chicago. Simmons' presence in the line-up inspired the White Sox to alter their park layout. They moved the diamond farther away from the screen to make certain Al's tremendous smashes need not travel so far to land in the stands.

Simmons paced the team to a sixth place 1933 finish, hitting .331, batting in 119 runs, and whacking 14 homers. Still, there hadn't been enough improvement to make Manager Fonseca confident of the future. Lew, now director of the major league's motion picture division, says, "I think I would have been dumped in the '33 season if we hadn't beaten the Cubs four in a row [3–2, 2–0, 9–0, 5–1] in the city series."

Fonseca was rehired for 1934, the first manager since the days of Kid Gleason to start a third consecutive season at the White Sox helm. But it proved to be a short season. Fonseca "quit by request" on May 8 in Washington.

Jimmy Dykes immediately was named to replace him. Jimmy was to enjoy a longer tenure than any White Sox manager and would come as close to working miracles as any mortal could.

When Dykes took over, he could expect little help from the scouting system, which, according to Fonseca, consisted "of a man and wife combination in Texas, and a San Francisco newspaperman." But Dykes did see some impressive newcomers on that '34 club. Zeke Bonura, a notorious fielder at first base, hit .302, .295, .330, and .345, in four White Sox seasons. Right-handers Vernon Kennedy, twenty-seven, and Monte Franklin Pierce Stratton, twenty-two, were promising.

In 1935, as the White Sox fought from the cellar to fifth, Ted Lyons won 15 and lost 8. Kennedy won 11, including a 5–0 no-hitter over Cleveland. Appling's .307, thirty-seven points short of Simmons' 1934 mark, gave him the club batting leadership.

And Luke soared to .388 in 1936, when for the first time since 1920 the White Sox landed in the first division. Now loyal South Side fans like J. C. Silvers and Earl Dunne had something to talk about — Appling's hitting and Kennedy's 21 victories. All winter they talked of Dykes, catcher Luke Sewell, infielder Tony Piet, second baseman Jackie Hayes, Bonura, and Dixie Walker. They talked of the 4–0 city series conquest and the future.

The third-place White Sox of 1936 won 81 and lost 70. Dykes' third-place White Sox of 1937 won 86 and lost only 68. Bill Dietrich, the right-hander who had come in from

Washington in 1936, pitched an 8–0 no-hitter against St. Louis on June 1, 1937. Monty Stratton topped the pitchers with 15–5.

In 1938 Stratton again was the team's most effective pitcher, winning 15 and losing 9. But Luke Appling broke a leg in training camp and Jackie Hayes and first baseman Joe Kuhel were handicapped with injuries, and pitchers Bill Dietrich and Clint Brown nursed sore arms. The Dykes men sagged to sixth, while the Cubs under Gabby Hartnett nailed down another pennant.

The hard luck that dogged the team did not end with the season. In November, while hunting near Greenville, Texas, Monte Stratton accidentally discharged a .32-caliber pistol, wounding himself in the right leg, piercing the femoral artery. Amputation was necessary. Though Stratton made a valiant comeback, a promising pitching career had been shattered.

If there was a particular bright spot in 1938, it was the acquisition of catcher Mike Tresh in a preseason swap for Dixie Walker. Tresh played in only ten games for the Sox in 1938, but he would be a bulwark for seasons to come.

Advent of the 1939 season filled owner John Louis Comiskey with excitement, for his White Sox were putting in lights at Comiskey Park. They were to use them for seven league games, and in the city series with the Cubs. J. Louis never was to see the White Sox under the lights. He died July 18, 1939. His widow, the spirited Mrs. Grace Comiskey, announced: "There must always be a Comiskey at the head of the White Sox. My son, Charley, grandson of the founder of the White Sox, will be fully fitted to operate the franchise when he reaches the proper age."

With timely hitting from Eric McNair (.324), Mike Kreevich (.323), Appling (.314), and Joe Kuhel (.300); with fine pitching from the winner of the first night game, John Dungan Rigney (15–8), Thornton Lee (15–11), Ted Lyons (14–6 and a 2.76 E.R.A.), and Clint Brown (11–10 in 61 games), the 1939 White Sox rose to fourth place.

WHITE SOX HALL-OF-FAMERS

CLARK C. GRIFFITH

...TED WITH MAJOR LEAGUE BASEBALL
...RE THAN 50 YEARS AS A PITCHER,
...ER AND EXECUTIVE. SERVED AS A
... OF THE CHICAGO AND CINCINNATI
... IN THE N.L. AND THE CHICAGO,
...YORK AND WASHINGTON CLUBS
...A.L. COMPILED MORE THAN 200
...ES AS A PITCHER, MANAGER OF THE
...NATI N.L. AND CHICAGO, NEW YORK
...SHINGTON A.L. TEAMS FOR 20 YEARS.

CHARLES A. COMISKEY
"THE OLD ROMAN"

STARTED 50 YEARS OF BASEBALL AS
ST. LOUIS BROWNS FIRST-BASEMAN IN 1882
AND WAS FIRST MAN AT THIS POSITION TO
PLAY AWAY FROM THE BAG FOR BATTERS. AS
BROWNS' MANAGER-CAPTAIN-PLAYER WON
4 STRAIGHT AMERICAN ASSOCIATION
PENNANTS STARTING 1885, WORLD CHAMPIONS
FIRST 2 YEARS. OWNER AND PRESIDENT
CHICAGO WHITE SOX 1900 TO 1931.

EDWARD ARTHUR WALSH
"BIG ED"

OUTSTANDING RIGHTHANDED PITCHER OF
CHICAGO A.L. FROM 1904 THROUGH 1916.
WON 40 GAMES IN 1908 AND WON TWO
GAMES IN THE 1906 WORLD SERIES. TWICE
PITCHED AND WON TWO GAMES IN ONE
DAY, ALLOWING ONLY ONE RUN IN
DOUBLEHEADER AGAINST BOSTON ON
SEPT. 29, 1908. FINISHED BIG LEAGUE PITCHING
CAREER WITH BOSTON N.L. IN 1917.

...YMOND WILLIAM SCHALK
CHICAGO A.L. 1912 TO 1928
NEW YORK N.L. 1929

...ER OF MAJOR LEAGUE RECORD FOR
...YEARS LEADING CATCHER IN FIELDING,
... YEARS; MOST PUTOUTS, NINE YEARS;
...ASSISTS IN ONE MAJOR LEAGUE (1810);
...CHANCES ACCEPTED (8965). CAUGHT
...NO-HIT GAMES INCLUDING PERFECT
GAME IN 1922.

THEODORE AMAR LYONS
CHICAGO A.L. 1923 TO 1946

ENTIRE ACTIVE PITCHING CAREER OF 21
SEASONS WITH CHICAGO A.L. WON 260
GAMES, LOST 230. TIED FOR LEAGUE'S MOST
VICTORIES 1925 AND 1927. BEST EARNED RUN
AVERAGE, 2.10 IN 1942 WHEN HE STARTED
AND FINISHED ALL 20 GAMES. PITCHED
NO-HIT GAME, AUG. 21, 1926 AGAINST BOSTON.
PITCHED 21-INNING GAME MAY 24, 1929.

Cleveland's Bob Feller tossed a no-hitter at the White Sox in the April 16, 1940, season opener at Comiskey Park. But with Appling hitting .348, and Taft Wright .337, the White Sox tied Boston for fourth. Then, surprise! They again won the city series.

The year 1940 was a fair one for the White Sox team. It was black for the veteran second baseman, Minter Carney (Jackie) Hayes.

Hayes suffered an eye inflammation during spring training. His major league career was terminated after eighteen regular season games, and he went blind. Almost a decade later the Sox, under the urging of Gene Kessler, Chicago *Sun-Times* sports columnist, played a benefit game for their little Jackie.

1941 produced a third-place finish and a four-straight city series victory over the Cubs. Thornton Lee's 22 wins paced the pitchers, who turned in 106 complete games. Taft Wright hit .322 and Appling .314.

Meanwhile Mrs. Grace Comiskey, who in 1940 had challenged the right of the First National Bank of Chicago to sell the club to ensure assets of the J. Louis Comiskey estate, was given complete command of the White Sox. In 1941, rebuffed in its efforts to force a sale, the bank resigned its stewardship. The Continental Illinois Bank, named as successor trustee in Comiskey's will, waived the right to sell. The door was open for Mrs. Comiskey and her family.

The players began the next season with attentions divided; the United States was at war. Taft Wright, injured in spring training, left for military service after 85 games in which he hit .333. Johnny Rigney broke even in six pitching decisions before putting on his sailor suit.

The 1942 Sox fell to sixth place. Ted Lyons (14–6) and John Humphries (12–12) bulwarked the pitching staff. Hampered by arm trouble, Thornton Lee won only two games, twenty less than in '41. Ed Smith, who had won 13 in '41, won but 7 and lost 20.

Season's end was marked by the final city series between

the Sox and their rich North Side neighbors. When that series was over, the regulars at McCuddy's and The Pump were lifting their toasts to the White Sox, who had won, four games to two.

In 1943 Jimmy Dykes elevated his charges to fourth place with 82 wins, and fell one-half game short of a tie for third. Appling won the batting crown with .328 and was second to Spud Chandler of the Yankees in balloting for the league's most valuable player. Elmer Ralph Hodgin, a combination infielder-outfielder, hit .314 against the wartime hurling. Guy Paxton Curtwright, thirty-year-old rookie outfielder, reeled off a consecutive game-hitting streak of 26 before Washington's Milo Candini and Alex Carrasquel finally stopped him on July 2. Right-hander Orval Grove won 15 games, Dietrich 12, and Edgar Smith 11. An added treat for White Sox fans was the base running of Wally Moses, a thirty-two-year-old speedster who had arrived from the Athletics the season before. He stole 56 bases.

In 1944, the up-again, down-again White Sox were down again — down in seventh place, though they had been second on June 25. Orval Grove and Bill Dietrich both posted a record of 14 and 16, Ed Lopat 11–10. Gordon Maltzberger, a relief specialist, won 10 and lost 5. Hodgins' .295 topped the hitters.

Tony Cuccinello, who had joined the Sox in 1943 after lengthy service in the National League, batted .308 to pace the Chicago hitters in the sixth-place season of '45. Cooch wound up his big-time playing career on that note, but eventually was to return to Chicago as coach of Manager Al Lopez's champion Go-Go White Sox.

1945 saw the departure of Harry Grabiner, front office standby since the days of the Old Roman. Grabiner was replaced by quiet, thoughtful Leslie O'Connor, long-time legal aide to Commissioner Landis, who had died in November, 1944. O'Connor's job as general manager of the White Sox would have been shunned by many prudent men, but it afforded Les a challenge, and more excitement than the paper work in the Commissioner's office.

The following months saw Bill Veeck, back from the wars, planning to sell the Milwaukee Brewers and once more viewing the White Sox with covetous eyes. He joined with Grabiner on a plan to bid for the White Sox. That plan never got off the ground, so the Veeck-Grabiner combine turned to Cleveland, where Veeck quickly astounded 'em with the wonders he could perform.

Meanwhile, Chicago manager Jimmy Dykes was finding it harder and harder to work even small wonders. His long managerial reign ended with the club in seventh place. Teddy Lyons was handed the job on May 25 and brought the '46 club home fifth (74–80). Lyons was given a lift by Appling's .309 average and by a record attendance of 983,403.

In 1947, though Ed Lopat won 16 games and Joe Haynes 14, the White Sox skidded to sixth. In fact, after the season was over the club skidded right out of the American League.

What brought this about was Les O'Connor's belief that he had found a loophole in the rule governing the signing of high school players. The White Sox legal eagle tested his belief by permitting Red Ormsby, the veteran umpire turned Chicago scout, to sign a sensational seventeen-year-old southpaw named George Zoeterman *before* he completed his studies at Chicago Christian, a private high school. Commissioner A. B. (Happy) Chandler, successor to Judge Landis, ruled that the White Sox had violated the rule protecting high school students. Chandler levied a $500 fine on the White Sox.

O'Connor refused to pay the fine. He contended that the rule was not applicable to Zoeterman because Chicago Christian was not a member of the National Federation of State High School Athletic Associations. Chandler's rebuttal was that the rule protected all high school students. When O'Connor refused to budge, Chandler suspended both him and the White Sox from Organized Baseball.

O'Connor fumed and fussed. He declared that the White

Sox would seek relief in federal court. The month of November, 1947, was just beginning, and it looked as if the baseball writers would have a busy and interesting winter.

But suddenly, from Minneapolis, young Charles (Chuck) Comiskey announced that the White Sox would pay. When he regained his composure, O'Connor offered to resign. The board of directors rejected his offer and he remained on until Lane was brought in following the 1948 season.

Zoeterman, meanwhile, had been ruled a free agent; all major league clubs except the White Sox were eligible to bid for him. He was landed by the Cubs, who never obtained any major league service from him.

Payment of the Zoeterman case fine brought the White Sox back into the American League — though not very far back. In 1948 they sustained 101 losses and came home an ignominious last. The high spot of the season came on July 18, in a game in Philadelphia, when portly Pat Seerey pounded out four home runs, two off Carl Scheib and one each off Bob Savage and Lou Brissie. Later, a night-game crowd of 51,013, drawn by Cleveland's Satchel Paige, helped swell season attendance to 777,844.

The cellar finish meant Lyons was out as manager. O'Connor was happy to get out as front office chief. Chuck Comiskey, who as early as spring training had warned of dire eventualities, announced that Ted had been succeeded by John Onslow and that Frank Lane was taking Les's post.

CHAPTER 9

Into the Age of Go

HEADMAN CHUCK COMISKEY, General Manager Frank Lane, and Manager John Onslow were major league rookies in their new posts as 1949 signaled the birth of a wonderful White Sox era. In time all three would get their wings clipped, but in the process it would be Lane who caused the most excitement.

Almost from the day he set foot in the fading Baseball Palace of the World, Frantic Frankie kept the pot boiling. A man dedicated to clearing away the old wood, the old ideas, and the old plumbing, soon he also became dedicated to clearing away Onslow, a hard-working fellow never particularly favored by the baseball gods.

However, Onslow, who was to lift the 1949 White Sox to sixth place, did not throw in the sponge the first time he suspected that Lane wanted to bring in a new manager. He battled back, and it was not until 1951 that Lane was able to turn the White Sox over to a field general of his choice, Paul Rapier Richards.

Lane's progress at clearing away the old player personnel and bringing in fresh faces was more immediate. On November 10, 1948, the first dip of his net brought in Walter William (Billy) Pierce, a southpaw slated for White Sox immortality. From that point on, Lane had 'em coming and going and with his wholesale trades and minor league forays was able to pull in such big ones as second baseman Nellie Fox, center fielder Jim Busby, shortstop Chico Carrasquel, slugger Gus Zernial, and lefties Bob Kuzava and Bob Wight. More came later.

Kuzava was 10–6 and Wight 15–13 under Onslow in 1949. Honest John's season might have been better had not Gus (Ozark Ike) Zernial, a 205-pound graduate of Hollywood in the Coast league, suffered a broken collarbone while making a circus catch on May 28.

Zernial made a marvelous comeback during the sixth-place campaign of 1950, which saw the venerable Red Corriden step up as interim manager following Onslow's exit late in May. Gus smashed out 29 home runs, an all-time White Sox season record.

The 1950 season also saw Pierce start to pay dividends with a mark of 12 won, 16 lost. Bob Wight came back with a 10–16 mark, and right-hander Ray Scarborough won 10. Phil Masi, the catcher who had moved over from Pittsburgh, worked 122 games. Hank Majeski hit .309 and Eddie Robinson .295.

Constantine (Gus) Keriazakos, a $60,000-bonus pitcher, lost his one pitching assignment and was soon to follow James Sloan Baumer, a $50,000-bonus shortstop who had vanished from the majors after appearing in eight games in 1949.

In 1950 Nellie Fox had an apprenticeship of 130 games, and left his employers with a maybe-yes, maybe-no attitude. Jim Busby, fleet twenty-three-year-old farm club product who was to inspire the "Go-Go" nickname, played in only 18 games with Chicago, spending most of the season in Sacramento.

But Alfonso Colon Carrasquel, the twenty-two-year-old Venezuelan shortstop, was a sensation with his glove work. This young nifty, pilfered from Branch Rickey, of all people, scarcely had arrived in training camp before presenting

Two old Sox pitching hands — Red Faber and Ted Lyons — get together in 1946.

evidence that he was to displace Aches-and-Pains Appling, who in the minds of many Chicagoans had been shortstop since Ol' Ab Doubleday invented baseball.

Appling made valiant attempts to fill in at first base and at second. Finally, on November 1, 1950, he gave way to younger legs and accepted managership of the Memphis farm club. The last of the old-line White Sox immortals had gone.

But with the passing of the old, the new had already arrived. Red Corriden had wound up the 1950 season, and Paul (the Genius) Richards was manager. Before the South Siders had forgotten their battle cry "C'mon Luke!" Richards and his gang would have them shouting "Go-go! Go-go! Go-go-go! Go-go, Chicago!"

1951 was at hand, and with the Go-Go White Sox topping the race for forty-four days, it was to be the most exciting season between the championship years of 1919 and 1959.

When he first began scanning the roster, Manager Richards had to smile as he reached the name of Chico Carrasquel. As manager of the Buffalo club, Richards had heard that Chico Carrasquel was burning up the diamonds of Venezuela. He determined to sign him for Buffalo, whence Chico would probably graduate to the Detroit Tigers. Richards was practically on his way to Venezuela to get Carrasquel when his Buffalo bosses said they did not want the Latin.

So Carrasquel slipped into the Brooklyn chain and was assigned to Fort Worth for his first and only season of minor league ball. There he was spotted by Frank Lane, the Chicago ivory-hunter.

Now, of course, when one saw a Dodger player and coveted him, he had to spar with the shrewd Mr. Rickey. That Lane did. Coyly he asked Branch to put price tags on several of his young players, expressing no particular interest in Chico at the time. Rickey reeled off some names and placed values on each. Soon Lane wired Rickey: ACCEPT YOUR TERMS ON CARRASQUEL. When Rickey protested that there

122   THE GO-GO CHICAGO WHITE SOX

had been no discussion of a swap, Lane refreshed his memory. A deal was a deal — or was it?

"I never fail to keep my word," Rickey said. Thirty-five thousand dollars and Fred Hancock, a rookie shortstop, went to the Dodgers for Chico.

Chico had no easy assignment trying to wrest a position from Appling. But his catlike fielding quickly won fans, and the *Chicago Tribune*'s Irving Vaughan, who rarely enthused about any ballplayer outside the Hall of Fame, compared him to Honus Wagner.

Richards, in his first season at the helm, saw Chico recognized as the American League's All-Star shortstop. Three more times Chico was to be the All-Star shortstop. Then he grew pudgy and perhaps careless. With his countryman Luis Aparicio waiting in the wings, Chico would go to Cleveland with Jim Busby in the 1955 deal that brought Larry Doby to Chicago. From Cleveland, he'd drift to Kansas City, then to Baltimore, which would cut him loose in December of 1959. So where did Carrasquel report for 1960 spring training? To Sarasota, Florida. There the White Sox club that had extended him a major league opportunity a decade before would be willing to give him a chance to hang on.

Back in 1951, with Chico already a one-year vet in the White Sox camp, Manager Richards began prodding Front Office Frankie to bring in two players with whom he had become fascinated. One was pitcher Saul Walter Rogovin, a dreamy right-hander who had toiled for Richards at Buffalo and who was going nowhere with the Tigers. The other was Orestes Saturnino (Minnie) Minoso, a youngster with Cleveland.

Lane had little trouble getting Rogovin from the Tigers for lefty Bob Cain, a winner of 9 and loser of 12 in 1950. Cain left Chicago with a 1–2 mark in '51 and added 11 triumphs and 10 losses at Detroit. Rogovin, who arrived from Detroit with a 1–1 mark for '51, recorded 11 victories and 7 losses for the Go-Go cause. Moreover, Saul was to win 14 and lose 9

in 1952. Though he'd not be around when the Sox completed
the long pull up championship hill, Rogovin must be rated
one of the first heroes of the Go-Go era.

The trade for Rogovin was accomplished with ease, but
Lane had to set all-time telephone records before winding up
the complicated swap that put Minoso in White Sox uniform
No. 9. The cost was high, with slugger Zernial part of the
price. As it turned out, Lane could have given twice what he
paid for Minoso and still wound up with an astounding bargain!

Now the Sox were a vital factor in the American League
scheme of things. In '51 Richards whipped them into a fourth-
place finish, and happy days seemed to be just around the
corner.

The Sox continued to wheel and deal for the next five seasons (1952-56), and even came up with two 20-game-winning
pitchers in Virgil Trucks and Billy Pierce. Minoso continued
to hit and run with the best in the business, Richards continued to juggle his thin line of talent, and the Sox continued
to stay among the upper echelon. But the Yankees were still
the Yankees (except for '54) and for five straight seasons the
Sox couldn't climb higher than third. It was a period of hope
and adjustment, but no advance.

In 1954 Richards quit near the close of the season and Marty
Marion, the old St. Louis Cardinal shortstop, was handed the
managerial reins. This was the season the Sox won 94 games,
their highest total in thirty-seven years, but still no pennant.
Marion hung around in 1955 and '56, and so did the Yankees.
The results were the same, and now the Comiskey Park
patrons became belligerent.

"Let's do something. Let's catch the Yankees. Third place
isn't good enough," was the cry from the stands, the front
office, the newspapers.

The next move? Bring in the only guy to have beaten the
Yankees in the reign of Casey Stengel.

And so from Cleveland the Sox acquired the masterminding

services of Al Lopez, another fellow who knew exactly how South Side fans felt. After all, hadn't Al been eating too much Yankee dust for too many years?

The good Señor was an immediate improvement. The Sox climbed a notch in 1957, to second place, their highest finish in thirty-seven years. New hope. New dreams.

"Now we're closer than ever," cried the South Side fans. But Lopez was to know more frustrations. It was no better in 1958 — in fact the Sox were never a serious factor. Even though they finished second again, there was still too much daylight between them and the Yankees. Now they were the Go-Go White Sox, but how far could they go?

The baseball world found out in 1959.

CHAPTER 10

The Heroes, 1

WHO'S ON FIRST? Earl Torgeson, or Ron Jackson, or Ray Boone, or perhaps Jim Rivera or Sherman Lollar? This was one of the major problems facing Manager Al Lopez late in February, 1959, when he left his plush new Tampa beach-front home — built on baseball earnings and oil well profits — to size up the White Sox checking in for spring training at Al Lopez Field.

Would Jackson, at twenty-five, finally begin to hit? There was some encouragement from Ted Williams' appraisal of the previous season: that the lanky first-sacker from Western Michigan College could develop into one of the game's feared power hitters. Defensively, though, Jackson showed little more skill than old Zeke Bonura. Some harsh critics, including baseball writer Dale Lancaster of the *Aurora Beacon-News*, suggested that for fielding they would have to take Bonura over Jackson, even now! So if Jackson was to clinch the first base job, he would have to convince Lopez that he could hit.

Other problems were on Lopez's mind, too. What about third base? Bubba Phillips, the converted outfielder obtained from the Detroit Tigers in exchange for Virgil Trucks, seemed the best bet. The peppery Phillips, a Little All-Amer-

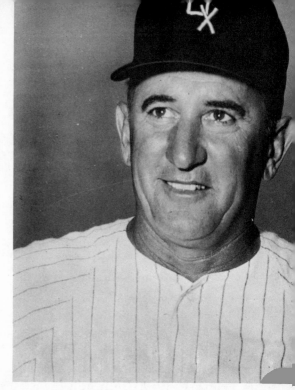

Al Lopez, a good guy who doesn't finish last.

ican halfback during undergraduate days at Mississippi Southern, had just turned twenty-nine. He had batted .273, .270, and .273 in three previous seasons, and before breaking a bone in his foot in June of 1958, he had seemed to be getting stronger with the stick. Best of all, Bubba had the kind of guts that Lopez admired.

Behind Phillips was Billy Goodman, a dependable left-handed hitter if not a distance clouter. On March 22 he would reach thirty-three. Besides Phillips and Goodman, there always was the good-fielding, light-hitting utility infielder, Chicago's own Sammy Esposito. Sammy had been a football and baseball standout at Fenger High School, on Chicago's far South Side. He had left Indiana University in 1952 to accept a White Sox contract offered by Doug Minor.

First base? Third base? And then there were those two

young men upon whom Lopez and the White Sox placed so
much faith — pitcher Barry Latman and outfielder John Callison. Would Latman and Callison be up to playing as front-
liners in their first full season in the majors?

There figured to be more pressure on Callison than on any
major league rookie outfielder since Mickey Mantle's debut
with the Yankees. Callison, an unassuming lad who was to
celebrate his twentieth birthday during this 1959 spring training season, had attracted White Sox scouts while a prep school
phenomenon in Bakersfield, California. Under orders to con-
centrate on quality rather than quantity, scouts Doc Bennett
and Hollis Thurston bore down on young Callison, and on
June 14, 1957, they got his signature on a White Sox contract.

Callison was sent to Bakersfield of the California League.
He punched out seventeen homers while batting .340. The
White Sox graduated him cum laude, moving him way up to
the Indianapolis American Association entry for 1958. John
met this challenge with twenty-nine homers and a .283 hitting mark, so when the American Association season ended,
he was rushed up to the parent club.

Callison's debut was in Comiskey Park on September 9,
1958, and the Red Sox were the oppposition. Sizing up big-
tent pitching for the first time, Callison wounded the Bos-
tonites with two doubles and a single. He played in eighteen
games and batted .297. The White Sox immediately tabbed
him as an outfield regular for 1959.

A fast windup with the White Sox in 1958 had won Latman, a husky right-hander closing in on his twenty-third
birthday, a chance as the fourth starter in a pitching corps
starring Early Wynn, Billy Pierce, and Dick Donovan.

Latman, another Californian, had broken in with the
Waterloo club in 1955. Then followed stops at Memphis and
Indianapolis and a brief trial in Chicago in 1957. During his
first stint with the Sox, Latman had won one and lost two, to
qualify for a return to Indianapolis. His 1958 campaign with
the Indians from the Hoosier state caused no one to forecast

that Barry would make 'em forget Teddy Lyons. Not with a mark of 9 victories and 11 losses and an earned-run average of 4.62.

But how Latman impressed them during that late '58 fling in Chicago! He was used in 13 games, won 3 and lost none, and wound up with a stingy 0.75 earned-run average. The big fast-baller had sold himself to Lopez. Latman himself exuded self-confidence.

Yet wasn't it asking too much of Callison and Latman to bear so much pennant pressure in their first full season? Lopez hoped not, but many believed it was. And as so often happens in baseball, the grandstand managers were to prove smarter than the field managers. Callison would be dispatched back to Indianapolis for extra seasoning, and big Barry would have difficulty getting established as a front-line starter.

And the season ahead promised more stumbling blocks than

Billy Pierce   Nelson Fox

first and third base and the youngsters to be brought along. There were the front office wrangles, and the New York Yankees. . . .

All in all, though, Manager Lopez had to admit he was a pretty lucky fellow. He did have going for him some White Sox stars coveted by managers in both leagues. Nellie Fox, for instance. At thirty-one, Nellie was the class of American League second basemen — the most famous and highest paid of the current Go-Go Sox.

Jacob Nelson Fox checked in on Christmas Day, 1927, in St. Thomas, Pennsylvania. His father, Jacob Fox, had been a sandlot player and would have liked a son of his to play in the majors. But in 1944, when Nellie asked to try out with Connie Mack's old Philadelphia Athletics in the wartime spring training base in Frederick, Maryland, Jake Fox was anything but enthusiastic. The boy was small and scrawny and a sophomore in high school.

With misgivings he loaded Nellie into the family truck and they drove to Frederick. There Jake told Connie Mack of his hopes that Nellie would return to St. Thomas Vocational High School to finish his education.

"A great idea," said Mack. "After all, he really is a little fellow."

But that afternoon Mack told Jake, "Your kid has baseball in his blood. Why don't you leave him with me?"

Jake shrugged and drove home alone.

The Athletics quickly shifted Nellie to a Class B club managed by that colorful former White Sox skipper, Lena Blackburne. Lena soon shipped Nellie to a Class D club. The young man was making progress — in the wrong direction.

In his debut in organized baseball Nellie hit .325 in 24 games with Lancaster. Later the same season he went to Jamestown and hit .304 in 56 games. Next season found him back in a Lancaster uniform, and the next, 1946, in Uncle Sam's khaki, in Korea. It was back to Lancaster in 1947. But '47 was an eventful year, for at season's end he was called up to the Athletics for a look-see. The Athletics didn't take much of a look — Nellie played only seven games and went to bat only three times. His average: .000.

The 1948 campaign at Lincoln, where he hit .311, proved all the apprenticeship Nellie needed to stick permanently in the big league. He played three season-end games for the Athletics in 1948, and was kept with the parent club in '49. Today Chuck Comiskey says that he first became interested in Nellie, and determined to get him, when Nellie was hustling for Lincoln. Frank Lane always claims the credit for himself, but readily admits that he had no suspicion of what a prize package he was taking from the Athletics. Both men agree that Fox might never have landed in Chicago had it not been for a feud between Chicago catcher Joe Tipton and Honest John Onslow, the outspoken Chicago manager of 1949 and part of 1950.

Onslow's White Sox had played the St. Louis Browns a doubleheader on May 1, 1949. Before they went down to defeat the Browns scored eight runs in the final inning of the nightcap. This infuriated Manager Onslow, and he assailed Tipton for some of the pitches called during the St. Louis uprising.

They nearly came to fisticuffs. Tipton became a permanent resident in the Onslow doghouse. A team joke was that Tipton was "the second-biggest fly in Onslow's ointment" — the biggest fly being Frantic Frankie Lane himself.

Then Onslow and Lane came to one of their rare agreements: They would trade off Tipton.

Lane had a chance to send Joe to Philadelphia for a second baseman who had hit .255 in 88 games with the 1949 Athletics. Lane grabbed Fox.

Nellie, who had been languishing in Pete Suder's shadow in Philadelphia, found himself overshadowed in Chicago by Cass Michaels, All-Star second baseman. But suddenly the shadow vanished: Lane shipped Michaels off in a package deal that brought in Al Kozar of Washington. Lane had ticketed Kozar as Michael's replacement.

Here Nellie Fox raised his hand, shifted his chaw of tobaccy to the other cheek, and protested: "Hey, what about me?"

Two things enabled Nellie to win the job. One was his constant hustling. The other was a back injury sustained by Kozar while hitting a homer against the Yankees. Nellie kept as busy as a fly in a sugar bowl trying to nail down his job as a regular; yet each time Frank Lane looked at the five-foot, eight-inch whirlwind, he would shake his head and make a mental note that Nellie was only a stopgap at second.

The same thought occurred to Paul Rapier Richards when Lane hired him as manager for 1951. Noting Nellie's size, his slim .247 batting mark of the previous season, and his inability to make the double play, Richards said, "Nellie doesn't figure."

Kozar hadn't figured, either. He had been shunted to the minors, and his fate awaited Fox if Richards could pull Eddie Basinski from the Pacific Coast League. Basinski couldn't be had. So when Richards assembled his White Sox for spring training in Pasadena, California, the second baseman was Nellie Fox.

Still Richards repeated, "Nellie doesn't figure."

Yet that very year Nellie Fox was to play in the All-Star game, and was to play in every All-Star game that followed, right through the pennant year of '59. Richards was to be the man mainly responsible, aside from Fox himself, for Fox's success.

Manager Richards' first concern was that "Little Bit," as Minnie Minoso called Nellie, was exercising too strenuously in Pasadena. Richards took stern measures to see that Fox got more rest than he needed — a mistake subsequently made by Richards' successor, Marty Marion. The late Edward Burns, a Chicago baseball writer, reported that Richards thought of stealing Fox's clothes and then locking him in quarters.

If spirited infield practice was going on, Richards would order Fox away. Nellie would scamper off, and the next time

Richards looked, he would be doing something twice as violent.

Meanwhile, Richards was moving to solve the other problems Fox presented. As Nellie later told it:

"I was Richards' No. 1 project in training camp. Joe Gordon, the former Yankee second baseman, came in to teach me defense. Coach Doc Cramer worked on my batting style, made me use a fatter bat. And Coach Ray Berres almost pitched his arm off giving me special batting practice. My big flaw was lunging into the ball and hitting off my front foot, with the left one hanging in the air.

"Richards worked hours with me on bunting. He made me hold the left hand loose to help deaden the ball and try to meet it with the end of the bat."

Fox proved an apt pupil. His average soared. He always got a piece of the ball, so that it became headline news whenever he struck out. And he was more than a left-handed menace to opposing pitchers. The "fragile" second baseman proved to be an iron man.

When the 1959 season began, Fox had played in 513 consecutive games, a record for major league second basemen. It was far in excess of the old mark of 477 consecutive games set by Eddie Collins, the mention of whose name still thrills old-time White Sox fans. This record was increased as Fox appeared in every 1959 White Sox game. Had Manager Marty Marion not asked him to rest on August 6, 1955, Fox's consecutive game streak at the conclusion of the regular 1959 season would have been 944!

"It was the most miserable day I ever spent in baseball," Fox said of his one-day layoff. Manager Marion added, "It was the most miserable day of my life, too — having to listen to him gripe on the bench."

There has been more to Fox's iron-man make-up than stamina. He has the courage to take on a lion.

"I remember a day in California in 1950," Coach Berres told us one evening around the hot stove. "We were playing

Barry Latman

Luis Aparicio

Jim Landis

Al Smith

the Pirates. A ground ball hit Nellie in the mouth, breaking off a tooth. We knew the pain was almost unbearable. Still, Nellie insisted on staying in the game."

In 1953, when the White Sox were in Washington, Nellie suffered leg injuries when four lockers fell on him. Trainer Ed (Doc) Froelich rushed to appraise damage. Fox grimaced: "Don't worry, vampire, I'll just spit on a little tobacco juice and everything will be okay."

Once Fox's keen eye failed him and he was hit on the elbow by a pitch from Yankee Tommy Byrne. Though the arm hung limp and required between-inning ice packs, Fox insisted on finishing the final three innings. No one figured Fox could avoid being out of action for a few days, except Fox.

The one injury that concerned Fox was self-administered. He fouled a batting-practice bunt, and the ball hit his eye. After four stitches were taken, Nellie ran to the mirror and pulled back the lid. "Was I glad to see this ugly old puss," he said.

When Fox's durability and tenacity are discussed, someone always brings up the block thrown on him by Yankee base runner Johnny Lindell. It was the worst jolt Fox ever took, and he fell unconscious. Two Yankee runs scored as the White Sox frantically tried to pry the ball free from Nellie's fingers.

No doubt it is Nellie's indestructibility that convinces most fans he's the oldest White Sox in point of service. Actually, Walter William (Billy) Pierce, his long-time roommate and most serious rival for affection of South Side fans, beat Fox onto the roster by one year. For a while, Billy Pierce was an even greater Chicago hero than Fox. Ironically, the White Sox were able to nail down the 1959 flag despite the fact that their ace left-hander had his worst season since the 1954 campaign, when he won nine and lost ten.

But before 1959 dealt unkindly with Pierce, he had done enough to establish himself as an all-time White Sox great who could be mentioned along with Eddie Collins, Cracker

Schalk, Ed Walsh, Teddy Lyons, and Luke Appling. Coming to Chicago from Detroit on November 10, 1948, along with $10,000 in exchange for aging catcher Aaron Robinson, Pierce had proved as good a bargain as Fox.

Like Fox, this lefty who tossed bullets (Ted Williams termed him "sneaky fast") had overcome a physical handicap — the suspicion of epilepsy. Like Fox, Billy was so young he could shave without a blade the first time he saw a major league training camp. Billy the Kid was only eighteen in 1945 when he appeared in five games for the Detroit Tigers, champions of the American League.

When Billy was a squeaky-voiced sixteen, Detroit's top catcher was a string-bean Texan named Paul Richards. They met in the elder Pierce's drugstore, a favorite hangout of some of the Tigers. Many times Billy and Richards talked baseball in that drugstore. A few short seasons later, both would be in Chicago White Sox uniforms — Pierce as a promising young lefty and Richards as a rookie major league manager rapidly becoming recognized as one of baseball's master tacticians.

The strange twist is that Pierce almost never made it to Chicago. Though he admits it most reluctantly, Frank Lane was not shopping for Pierce when the negotiations with Detroit were under way; he coveted Ted Gray, another young Tiger pitcher. But Tiger officials insisted on keeping Gray and peddling Pierce.

The deal drew an editorial blast from a Detroit newspaper. As Billy developed, there was continued gnashing of teeth among Motor City folk. He posted a 1.97 earned-run average in 1955, then spun twenty victories in both 1956 and 1957. Lefty Gray, meanwhile, never lived up to that early promise and was plagued with arm trouble. Gray eventually joined Pierce on the White Sox roster in December, 1954, when Frank Lane put across a thirteen-player swap involving the Tigers and Orioles. Gray pitched in only two games for the Sox in '55, neither a decision, and was destined to spend the rest of his career wandering around the league on waivers.

The Pierce larceny perpetrated upon Detroit was recalled anew when, during the most torrid weeks of the 1959 pennant race, young right-hander Bob Shaw took up the slack caused by Pierce's slump. Tiger fans were well aware that Shaw had been Detroit property until June 15, 1958 — when he and infielder Ray Boone were traded to the Sox in exchange for outfielder Tito Francona and pitcher Bill Fischer.

No doubt of it, Bill Pierce has been a great one. Through the 1959 campaign, he accounted for 165 major league victories — all but three of them for the White Sox. And experts assert that Pierce would already have 200 games if he weren't such a nice fellow.

It is no secret that Pierce refused to brush back the players who crowded the plate. Georgie Myatt, former White Sox coach, explained, "There's just one fault with Billy as a pitcher. He refuses to throw close when the batters cheat."

This admirable fault has hardly pleased Billy's bosses. Frank Lane threw a fit when Cass Michaels — then with the Athletics — touched Pierce for the bases-filled hit that defeated the White Sox. In the Chicago dressing room, Frank demanded, "Why the devil didn't you loosen up Michaels with some close ones?"

"I couldn't throw close to Cass," said Pierce. "We're friends."

Lane left, muttering to himself. Later he passed one of those fine old Irish ladies in the army of White Sox fans. She told sportscaster Vince Garrity, "Glory be to Heaven, but Mr. Lane's resigned from the Holy Name Society again!"

It was in the spring of 1959, in Tampa, that I finally asked Billy Pierce about his reluctance to brush back a batter. Good-looking Billy, his hairline receding now, was in the Al Lopez Field locker room after lobbing a few innings of a practice game. A serious expression replaced his smile as he pondered my question. Finally he said, "Let's just say that I'm the way I am. I love to play baseball, but I don't want to risk hurting anyone just to chalk up a win. When I leave, I want to remember that I played the game the way it was supposed to be played — as a game. I'll have to live with myself after I've been forgotten as a White Sox pitcher.

"Here's what I mean, but I don't want you to use it in the *Chicago Tribune*. Remember my game with Washington early last year?"

I nodded. How could any White Sox fan forget that Pierce masterpiece?

It was the night of June 27, 1958, in Comiskey Park. Billy was toiling on the mound for Chicago, and he was magnificent. Inning after inning he set down the Senators without a hit. Early they were victimized by his curve ball. Later, he began coming in with what once had been the livest fast ball in the American League. This night, Billy Pierce seemed almost as fast as ever.

During the closing innings, there was a restless roar from the stands each time Pierce cranked up in his distinctive rhythmic style, hunched the left shoulder, and fired another pitch. Behind the plate, Sherman Lollar was praying. It could be more than a no-hitter! It might be the best-pitched White Sox game since Charley Robertson shackled the Tigers on April 30, 1922.

Defensively, the White Sox had rallied around their ace. Lu Aparicio made a spectacular stop on Rocky Bridges in the fourth. In the sixth, Billy Goodman snared a boomer off Ken Aspromonte's bat and shot down the speeding Senator at first base. The seventh inning saw first baseman Earl Torgeson stretch to make an unbelievable catch on Goodman's throw as Roy Sievers scooted toward first.

Now, with two out in the ninth, Comiskey Park was echoing with one great sustained cheer. The Washington batter was Ed FitzGerald, pinch-hitting for pitcher Russ Kemmerer. Billy Pierce was one out from becoming the first to hurl a perfect game since Yankee Don Larsen in the 1956 World Series. There was only one out to go before Billy Pierce got the thirteenth White Sox no-hitter in the club's storied history.

He was about to add his name to an illustrious list that had Jimmy Callahan's name (1902) at the top and Bob Keegan's name (1957) at the bottom.

Swinging late on Pierce's first pitch, FitzGerald sliced the knee-high curve down the first base line — fair by only a foot and barely beyond the grasp of Ray Boone, now subbing at first.

No matter that Albie Pearson was retired immediately to preserve Pierce's 3–0 shutout. The shutout couldn't ease his heartache, but in the dressing room Billy forced a smile and said, "I was happy to win."

Yes, I remembered that game, and I was sure Billy had wished a thousand times that he could have back that one bad pitch to Ed FitzGerald.

"I wanted that no-hitter," Billy went on. "I'd like to have a perfect game more than anything else in the world. But if I had to do it over again — if I knew that throwing at Ed Fitz-Gerald would get me the perfect game — I still wouldn't take the chance. Look, I'm not criticizing any other pitcher, I'm just being Billy Pierce."

Walter William Pierce, born in Detroit on April 2, 1927, turned his first serious attention to baseball ten years later. As he tells it: "I refused to have my tonsils removed. My folks offered me a major league baseball and a good glove if I'd have the operation. I took the payola. It really was a thrill to throw around that 'league' ball. I started as a sandlot first baseman, but my first and greatest baseball hero was Tommy Bridges, the old-time Tiger pitcher who also was a little fellow. While I was growing up around Detroit I dreamed of being a Tiger."

Young Billy dreamed of playing football at the University of Michigan, where he figured to study medicine. But gradually, as his fast-balling became the talk of Detroit, he found himself concentrating more and more on baseball.

As a junior in 1944, Billy pitched six shutouts for suburban Highland Park High School. He was named to play in the

East-West All-Star boys' game and was chaperoned to New York by Dale Stafford, then sports editor of the *Detroit Free Press* and now publisher of the Greenville, Michigan, *News*. Stafford once told me, "I never saw such a clean-living youngster. On our trip to New York for the East-West game, Billy kept a diary. One morning I found it open to this entry: 'Here it is ten o'clock and Mr. Stafford still hasn't gone to bed.'"

Billy was named the most valuable player in that 1944 game. With the honor came a four-year college scholarship. Prompted by scout Wish Egan, the Tigers acted quickly to snare the youngster. Pierce gave up the scholarship and forgot medical school to sign a contract.

When it came time for 1945 spring training, Billy left high school and headed to spring training. He still hadn't reached his eighteenth birthday!

Billy was assigned to Buffalo's International League team, managed by Bucky Harris. He won only 5 and lost 7, compiling an earned-run average of 5.42. Season's end found Billy in a Detroit Tiger uniform while the Tigers closed in on their World Series engagement with the Chicago Cubs. Now he was a teammate of catcher Paul Richards, who was running out his major league string. Richards immediately began counseling the fast but erratic southpaw. Richards was to continue tutoring him at Buffalo, then with the White Sox. Now Billy admits, "Richards taught me practically everything I know about pitching. He showed me how to throw a slider and improved my pitching 100 per cent."

Charles Leo (Gabby) Hartnett, the Chicago Cubs' Hall of Fame catcher, was Pierce's manager at Buffalo in 1946. A back injury held Billy back; he pitched in only ten games, won three and lost four. Richards turned up at Buffalo as playing-manager in 1947, and Pierce rebounded with a 14–8 mark.

The jump to the Tigers came in 1948. At season's end, after appearances in twenty-two games, Billy had won three and lost none. By one form of mathematics, 3 and 0 is perfect. Yet the Tigers, studying Billy's horrendous 6.38 earned-run average, figured their wild lefty was less than perfect and were willing to put him on the block when Frank Lane, new general manager of the White Sox, began shopping around for his first big-league swap. Many still believe that Lane's first deal is his monument.

Frantic Frankie himself was soon awed by the southpaw's spectacular success. Once, when pressed to explain how so much speed could come from a pitcher of only 175 pounds, program weight, and perhaps five pounds less by honest measure, Lane said, "Like Bantam Ben Hogan, Billy has co-ordination, marvelous co-ordination. He gets everything behind his pitches; no waste motion."

Billy Pierce pitched seven White Sox openers through 1959, but he'll never forget the first one. He beat the Browns in St. Louis, 17–3. "Besides the thrill of winning, I remember two things about that game. First, because it was such an important start for me. Second, I remember a double play started by Nellie Fox, who made an almost impossible throw to Chico Carrasquel at second. Chico doubled the hitter at first. We were leading by only two or three runs at the time, and I've often wondered what the outcome might have been if Fox hadn't choked off that St. Louis rally.

"It's strange, isn't it, that I remember very little about beating Cleveland in Comiskey Park in the 1956 opener — yet I still can see the next day's game, when Jack Harshman beat Herb Score and the Indians, 1–0. Brother, that was a cold day! Score had a no-hitter going, even after our run. Score could have pitched a no-hitter and still lost it!

"My toughest winning opener — until another one comes along — was in 1957, at Cleveland. We won, 3–2, but I had to go eleven innings against Score. Probably my outstanding memory of that game is that I doubled in a White Sox run."

The season of 1955 Pierce remembers for more than yielding opening-day honors to Virgil Trucks, and for more than his 1.97 earned-run average. "Yes, I lost four 1–0 games — and still won fifteen."

During his long career with the White Sox, Billy Pierce has found more rewards than hard-earned pitching victories and boxcar-figure pay checks. He has found thousands of fans. The unofficial Pierce Fan Club ranges from Comiskey Park bleacherites to such box-seat regulars as realtor Les Price and Mayor Daley; from Dan Ryan, president of the Cook County Commission, to industrialist Titus Haffa and Mrs. Haffa; from young John Roscich, who in 1959 realized the ambition of being White Sox bat boy in the World Series, to Mrs. Gloria McCreadie Pierce, Billy's high school sweetheart and mother of three little Pierces.

Roscich gave me this appraisal of Pierce in 1957: "Billy's always thinking of others. He worries when some of the deserving White Sox aren't named to the All-Star team. When he sends me for a bottle of pop or a candy bar, he buys me one, too. He's absolutely a nice guy."

The Pierces, Billy and Gloria, are baseball's All-American couple. Sitting around one spring training afternoon at the Pierce cottage, Gloria confided her great pride in Billy's many appearances in the All-Star game.

"Yes, she's my fan now," said Pierce, "but I can remember when she said her biggest thrill in baseball would be to get Ted Williams' autograph. Anyhow, she's not only a loyal fan, but a smart one, and there was the day I had to go to Marty Marion — he was the White Sox manager then — and tell him that he'd better change our bunt sign because Gloria had stolen it, so very likely the opposition would be stealing it too. But I'm glad Gloria likes baseball; it's quite a topic of conversation for us. There's only one question she's forbidden to bring up."

"Yes," said Gloria. "I'm never to ask, 'Honey, why didn't you give Mickey Mantle a curve instead of the fast ball?'"

Billy Pierce and $10,000 for Aaron Robinson or Nellie Fox for Joe Tipton — which was the greater steal? The White Sox fans gathering around Red McNamara's and Ed O'Leary's, and Harry Morini's Corona, The Pump, and Ned Cord's, and

Friendly Frank Frifield's, will be arguing that question until Lollar steals home from second.

The acquisition of either Pierce or Fox would have made Frank Lane's tenure with the club a profitable one. But Lane was constantly turning up embryo stars in unlikely places; and over six years ago he hit the mother lode down in Venezuela, whence had sprung the uncorpulent Chico Carrasquel.

This second outstanding Venezuelan was, like the first, a shortstop. His name — Luis Aparicio. He was born in Maracaibo on April 29, 1934; and despite a few hints that he might retire when he's twenty-eight, he entered the 1960 season with promise of many great campaigns ahead of him. Indeed, it seems likely that before loose-limbed Luis hangs up his spikes he will be recognized as the greatest fielding shortstop of all time. That would make Aparicio Lane's most valuable contribution to the Go-Go Sox.

Frank sounded off early in '55 about Lu. "This kid Aparicio down in Memphis — he could make you forget Carrasquel. He's like a cat. We had him at Waterloo in '54, and he hit .282. I don't think he'll be hitting .282 in the majors, but his glove will carry him. The White Sox have had a tradition for great shortstops, even before Luke Appling and Chico Carrasquel. This kid'll continue that tradition."

Despite Lane's enthusiasm, there were some in the White Sox family who remained unsold on Aparicio. In January of 1956, with Lane gone to the St. Louis Cardinal front office and Chico Carrasquel preparing to try on his new Cleveland Indians' uniform, Nellie Fox ventured to the Chicago press: "Aparicio must be quite a ballplayer, but have people forgotten about Jim Brideweser? I thought he did a great job last season when he filled in for Chico. Naturally, I'm just giving a personal opinion — Marty Marion will decide on the shortstop."

Manager Marion was no more enthusiastic. As 1956 spring training sessions got under way in Tampa, he would shake his head over the shortstop situation. Charles Comiskey and

Johnny Rigney put their confidence in Aparicio. Slats Marion, whose brilliance in the St. Louis Cardinal infield had earned him the name of "Mr. Shortstop," was going to give Brideweser and Carl (Buddy) Peterson a shot at Carrasquel's job.

Marion frequently voiced his misgivings as we sat around in the White Sox refreshment room, on the third floor of the Tampa Terrace Hotel, with Howard West, coaches George Myatt, Don Gutteridge, Ira Hutchinson, and Ray Berres, and newspapermen Leo Peterson, Joe Reichler, Jack Hand, the seriously ailing Gayle Talbot, Milton Richman, and Arthur Richman of New York; Bobby Hicks and Bob Hudson of Tampa; Shirley Povich and Francis Stann of Washington; Cleveland's Gordon Cobbledick, and the full Chicago crew including John Hoffman and Gene Kessler of the *Sun-Times*, Warren Brown and Leo Fischer of the *American*, John Carmichael and Bud Nangle of the *Daily News*, and Edward Prell of the *Tribune*.

Once Marion said, "Aparicio has a floppy glove, a lot like a first baseman's. He can dive for spectacular catches, but the glove dangles off his fingers. On the slow grounders I can't see how he can get solid contact with the ball. I'm going to ask him to use a glove small enough to feel a ball."

Marion also saw that as Aparicio made the double-play pivot he was shying from base runners steaming into second. Marion said, "He'll have to learn to throw that ball right at their heads and make them duck."

Still, as practice went on, Marion came to suspect that Aparicio was something special, after all. There was one way to find out in a hurry — start Aparicio at shortstop in the exhibition opener against Cincinnati.

This proved a rewarding experiment. Aparicio scored the winning run from second while Jim Rivera was forcing Sandy Consuegra. Marion exclaimed, "As Paul Richards would say, that kid runs like a scalded dog!" Two seasons later, trainer Ed (Doc) Froelich looked back to Aparicio's training camp debut and said, "I've seen lots of baseball in my days with the

Cubs, the Yanks, and Red Sox, and now with the White Sox, but since the first time I saw him run the prettiest sight in the game has been watching that graceful little Looey scoring from second on a single!"

Casey Stengel, the Yankees' canny manager, once observed that his Mickey Mantle could run across the grass without bending it. Ol' Case well might have made the same observation about Aparicio, and early in Lu's career he did say, "That little fellah gets balls your other fellah [Carrasquel] never coulda reached!"

Loud approval of Aparicio began pouring in almost from the minute Marion started him in that first exhibition. Soon Luis' great glove work and daredevil base running won Marion over. Soon, too, Marion learned that Aparicio could take rough play. It was in an exhibition with the Yankees, and the New Yorkers' Billy Martin charged into second base with spikes high, nicking Señor Aparicio. Between innings Luis took inventory of the damage and reassured his White Sox mates: "Don't worry — my chance at heem come pretty queeck!"

It did, and so did Aparicio's success. Besides making unbelievable fielding stops look commonplace, he led the American League in base stealing in 1956, again in 1957, 1958, and 1959! During 1959, Chicago was the only place you would find much of an argument against labeling Aparicio the greatest contemporary shortstop. The argument came from Chicago Cub fans very partial to their home run slugger, Ernie Banks. Bill Veeck injected himself into the friendly controversy by declaring he wouldn't trade Aparicio for Banks even if the Cubs threw in Wrigley Field.

By the time Little Looey had helped pace the White Sox to the '59 flag, Venezuelans were forced to agree that Luis Ernesto Aparicio, Jr., was a greater shortstop than Chico Carrasquel, or even greater than Luis Ernesto Aparicio, Sr., who spurned a chance with the Washington Senators when Junior was five years old.

The meteoric rise of Luis Ernesto Aparicio, Jr., began when he was a nineteen-year-old playing with the Cardenales of Barquisimeto, Venezuela. It was set off by the concern of the Maracaibo professional Gavilanes, co-owned by Uncle Ernesto Aparicio and Luis Sr., over Dad Aparicio's aging legs. Manager Ralph (Red) Kress, on lend-lease to the Gavilanes from his coaching job with the Cleveland Indians, wondered why the Gavilanes couldn't snatch young Luis from the Cardenales and retire Luis Sr.

Uncle Ernesto and Luis Sr. shrugged and said Little Looey was only a boy. Kress argued that no one ever had been known to get to the top in pro baseball without making a start, and the sooner the better.

Uncle Ernesto and Luis Sr. yielded. Luis Jr. was summoned to replace his pappy as the Gavilanes shortstop. The big night was November 18, 1953, and, of course, the Latins had to do it up with a fanfare that would have impressed even Bill Veeck. The elder Aparicio and his talented young son went to the shortstop position. There Aparicio Sr. handed his glove to Little Looey. Then the father embraced his son, gave him a blessing, and forsook the position. The older order had yielded to the new.

Young Aparicio showed more than Manager Kress had dared expect. He was not far from a debut in the United States.

According to Edward Prell, the *Chicago Tribune*'s senior baseball writer, Kress quickly tipped off Cleveland's general manager, Hank Greenberg, about the unpolished teen-ager. The Indians sent their ace talent scout, Cy Slapnicka, to pass judgment. Prell reports that Slapnicka caught up with the Gavilanes at a game in Caracas. Slapnicka called for a huddle with Dad Aparicio, Uncle Ernesto, and Kress. A sports writer named Eduardo Moncada, fluent in English and Spanish, was the moderator.

Uncle Ernesto was the Aparicio spokesman and asked $10,500. The deal appeared set, but Slapnicka said he needed

Greenberg's approval. Hank instead suggested that Aparicio be sent to an Indian camp in the United States. If he liked the looks of Luis after close inspection, the Indians would pay $5,250. Against this offer, the Aparicios had to gamble Junior's transportation to the United States — and back if Greenberg said no.

Meanwhile, Frank Lane had gotten wind of the major league potential of Luis Ernesto, Jr. His spies were Pablo Morales, owner of the Caracas club; Lum Harris, a White Sox coach who managed for Morales; and Chico Carrasquel, the native son who wintered in the Caracas infield. But then Harris gave Lane the sad news that Cleveland apparently had taken title to the youthful shortstop.

According to Prell, Lane read the riot act to Morales. The Caracas team could not have Carrasquel for the next winter season unless Lane got Aparicio, pronto. In exchange, the White Sox were prepared to pay $6,000 for Luis' contract, and to pay him $4,000 to play for one of their farm clubs in the United States.

The senior Aparicio was by the side of Pablo Morales, Prell wrote in *The Saturday Evening Post*, during the heated long-distance telephone negotiations with Frank Lane. Confronted with Lane's offer, Lane's oratory, and Lane's threats to Morales, Luis Sr. said the Venezuelan equivalent of "okay." Acceptance of the offer was telegraphed to Lane. All the ramifications of the negotiations never were explained, but apparently Little Looey was satisfied. The 1954 season found him outfitted in the uniform of Waterloo, Iowa, Chicago's Three-I League farm. He batted .282 and graduated to Memphis, where next year he hit .273.

When the Memphis club and all its players were sold late in 1955, the White Sox cannily followed up on arrangements to purchase Aparicio from the new owners, who included Ned Buring and Leo Burson. Then the White Sox sent Aparicio a contract which came back unsigned. This was the first hint that Luis had a mind of his own. And Luis Ernesto Aparicio, Jr., kept sending contracts back unsigned until the price was right.

He hit .266 in 152 games for Marion's 1956 White Sox. At season's end, balloting for the American League rookie-of-the-year was a formality like a Russian election. Aparicio collected 22 of 24 votes. Tito Francona, then with Baltimore, and Cleveland's Rocky Colavito drew a single vote each.

And the White Sox and Venezuela had a new hero. Carrasquel was almost forgotten.

Another young speedster who lent so much *Go!* to the 1959 White Sox was James H. Landis, born in Richmond, California, on March 9, 1934. Landis took longer to establish himself as a major-leaguer, perhaps because of two seasons spent in military service; but late in that tight campaign of '59 Detroit broadcaster George Kell said, "If I had to name the most valuable player on the White Sox, I would have to think a long while before passing up Jim Landis."

Landis had drawn equal praise only a few days after Manager Lopez began putting the '59 Go-Go crew through its spring paces. A warm Florida sun bathed Al Lopez Field that particular morning, and Donie Bush took refuge in the locker room. Hands in pockets, he paced the concrete floor, berated modern-day players, lamented the passing of outfielders who could throw like those of the Donie Bush-Ty Cobb era. Suddenly Bush paused to watch Jim Landis scamper from the room. Bush pointed to Landis. "I said it, but I was a bit wrong. That kid can throw like the old-timers. He can throw you out at the plate."

The 1959 opinions voiced by Kell and Bush were more certain than the one held by Manager Lopez several times during that frustrating spring of the previous year. In fact, he came very close to giving up on him. As he later told me, "It was tough to go along with Landis when our club was sagging and he was hitting under .200. Sure, as a defensive center fielder he was better than almost anyone in baseball, but as Rogers Hornsby says, you can shake great fielders out of the trees — it's the hitters that are hard to come by.

"Then, early in June of '58, Landis began slapping the ball with authority. He had one fifteen-game streak when he hit .404. Wound up with .277; only Nellie Fox had a higher average. Landis led the Sox in total bases with 227. And he was second in runs batted in, homers [15], and slugging."

Lopez had almost given up on Landis, yet he kept giving him every chance. And just when Lopez's patience was being strained, Landis delivered. Jim's sensational play in 1959 justified Lopez's faith and judgment; and many times since as he was golfing in Tampa and St. Petersburg and Clearwater, Al has broken into a cold sweat at the thought of how close he came to losing his center fielder.

What, besides time and the patience of Lopez, had been responsible for the maturing of Landis? The question was put to Landis himself during spring training in Tampa.

Landis said, "Let's start at the beginning. First of all, I wanted to play ball ever since I was a kid. My dad had been an amateur boxer, and I sparred a lot with him; but baseball was my first interest, and when I was in high school I played second and third base. Our doctor stopped me from playing basketball because he said all the jumping would be too much of a strain on my knee.

"See, when I was about three, I suddenly was unable to walk. I had a knee operation, and regained use of the leg. But even through high school, the knee would go out on me.

"After high school, I went to Contra Costa Junior College. We had played our third or fourth game when a White Sox scout — Bob Mattick — asked if I'd be interested in a pro contract. I listened and was impressed by Mattick. He was a gentleman who didn't make any rash promises. Just told me what would be expected, and what I possibly might do. I felt Mattick was a man I could trust. So when Hollie Thurston backed up Mattick with a contract for $2,500, I signed.

"I quit school, promising myself that someday I would get my degree in physical education, and joined the Colorado Springs club in training at Victoria, Texas. After training, I joined the Wisconsin Rapids club and took the third base job when the regular was released. Then the White Sox had a special camp for rookies. There I met Johnny Mostil, who was field supervisor of the farm system. I knew that Mostil had been one of the game's outstanding center fielders, and I was flattered when he tried me in center. His pointers were invaluable.

"He lectured me and showed me. He taught me how to get the jump on a ball, how to take a ball off the wall, and how to throw to cut off a runner. He worked us so hard that once Richards had to tell him to stop."

After a year at Colorado Springs (he hit .313 and was voted the league's most valuable player) and two in the army, Landis was more than a novice athlete when he reported to Manager Marion in February, 1956. Marion was impressed, and sitting around with Bud Nangle, John Carmichael, Bob Elson, Don Wells, Warren Brown, Ed Prell, John Hoffman, and the rest of us in the lobby of the Tampa Terrace Hotel, he would often praise Landis's speed and his slingshot throwing arm.

But Landis wasn't ready for the big jump. He was sent to Colorado Springs when the 1956 training camp broke up. There he hit .429 in 13 games to graduate to Memphis. Memphis used him in 92 games. Facing better pitching than at Colorado Springs, and his bat still rusty from the inactivity in Alaska, Landis hit only .257. Still, at the season's end the White Sox purchased his contract.

Jim says, "The pressure was on me, I knew, when I came to camp in 1957. The question in my mind, and I know it was in the mind of our new manager, Al Lopez, was — could I hit big-league pitching?

"I divided that season between Chicago and Indianapolis. It was rough. My wife, Sandra, realized it was rough and tried

to be encouraging. I hit .212 for the White Sox in ninety-six
games, and .246 during my time in Indianapolis. During the
winter, I came to realize that if I was to stay up in 1958, I
would have to hit for the average. I was worried, naturally.

"I began looking for help as soon as we got to Tampa. One
who gave it to me was Early Wynn, who had just come over
from the Indians. He had been one of the great pitchers on a
Cleveland staff that caused me so much trouble in '57, so I
asked Early how they got me out. Wynn said the Indians got
me by pitching bad balls, high and tight, inside. I was biting
on those bad pitches.

"So I made up my mind to be more selective. I had two
rules: one, try to be quick with my hands, and two, follow
the ball!

"Because Nellie Fox was such a good hitter, they suggested
he help me — on bunting, particularly. But Nellie, wonderful guy, talked 'em out of it. He was afraid he would just
confuse me more, because Nellie is a left-handed hitter and
I'm right-handed.

"Ron Northey, who was quite a hitter, stepped in to give
me some tips in '58 spring training. Northey and Lopez suggested a change in my batting grip. They told me to keep
moving into the pitch.

"Study hitters? Actually there's only one hitter I've ever
studied — Ted Williams. I love to watch Ted Williams hit.
Never, even in batting practice, does he go for a bad ball. If
ever there was a hitting artist, it was Williams.

"I didn't ask Williams for tips. Who was I to bother Ted
Williams? He was ready for the Hall of Fame and I was just
a rookie. I couldn't get courage to talk to him.

"Now, you asked me how I finally began hitting for the
average, just when Lopez was ready to give up. I guess first
of all, everything I had been told began to take hold. Then
I was playing every day, and my timing was improving. I tell
you what I believe finally made the difference: after going

up, day after day, I finally became relaxed. More important, I got that feeling of belonging.

"Yes, after that my hitting perked up. You see, I was awed by being up with all the great major-leaguers I had been reading about. When I finally came to realize they were just guys like myself, I regained my confidence. I knew I belonged."

The lean six-footer felt he belonged early in 1958; he proved it in 1959. As Coach Don Gutteridge explained, "Maybe Landis never will be a Ted Williams or Stan Musial at the plate, but he hits solidly, and dangerously. Day after day, he makes catches look easy. We hit the same thing against other teams and they fall in for hits. But Landis is such a serious guy, and goes about his business so quietly, that no one pays any attention. Talk about your most valuable player — he's it."

As baseball closed out the fantastic 50's, the whip-armed speed-boy looks forward to bigger headlines, fatter pay checks, and more World Series dividends. But until he reads these lines, Landis will not be aware of an incident preceding a Boston Red Sox-White Sox game in Comiskey Park in June of 1958. Big Ron Jackson, whom the White Sox swapped to Boston for pitcher Frank Baumann following the 1959 championship, had Ted Williams cornered for hitting advice. Williams told Jackson, "Of course you can be a big-league hitter. I know it. You have what it takes, if you'll just work at it. On the other hand, I don't think your teammate — Jim Landis — ever will catch on to hitting this big-time pitching. Only don't tell him that. He's a swell kid and I wouldn't do anything to hurt his confidence because a fellow at the plate needs all the confidence he can get."

By the time spring training came around in 1959, of course, it was too late to hurt Landis's confidence. He had arrived. Landis was of star stature, like Fox, Pierce, and Aparicio. No wonder Al Lopez's optimism outweighed his doubt. 1959 was to be The Year!

CHAPTER 11

The Heroes, 2

A SCATTERING of Tampa folk were already in the stands when Al Lopez strode onto the field to start 1959 spring training. Standing against the signboard fence, he scanned the seats and saw his long-time friends, Charley Gregory of The Fort and Joe Valdes of Spanish Park, Howard West of the Tampa Terrace and Tommy Donofrio of the Club Rio, and perhaps a dozen others.

Then Al turned to the field, studied pitchers Early Wynn and Dick Donovan, and catcher Sherman Lollar. Wynn and Donovan, with Pierce, figured to be the pitching front-liners. As for Lollar, who could say that any backstop in the league was better than Chicago's General Sherman?

Early (Gus) Wynn, the calculating right-hander, was born in Hartford, Alabama, on January 6, 1920. He came to Chicago with Al Smith in the deal that sent Minnie Minoso and Fred Hatfield to Cleveland. After winning 14 and losing 17 at Cleveland in 1957, when he led the American League in strike-outs with 184, Early won 14 while losing 16 in his first season with the Sox, again topping the circuit in strike-outs with 179. He had been the winning pitcher in the '58 All-Star game; he owned 249 pitching triumphs, highest total of any player still active in the majors, and he'd just arrived from his home in Nokomis, Florida, in his private plane.

At thirty-nine Early hoped to have a good year or two left. But if someone could have told him that in 1959 he'd win the Cy Young Award as the top pitcher in the majors, he probably would have laughed. After eighteen years in the majors, a man was bound to slow down. . . .

The year was 1936, and Early wasn't quite seventeen, when his long career began. The Washington Senators were holding a tryout camp in Sanford, Alabama, and a shy young man with some Indian blood in his veins had trekked over from the family home in Hartford, Alabama, to see what his chances were. His leg still sore from a football fracture, the youngster waited almost an eternity before Washington's Clyde Milan noticed him and called, "Hey, kid! What're you?"

"I'm a pitcher," said the kid.

"A pitcher?" Milan grinned. "Who told yuh that?"

"My father."

That prompted the Senators to give Wynn a tryout. Come next season — 1937 — he was pitching for Washington's Sanford farm in the Florida State League. He won 16 and lost 11. By the latter part of 1939, after additional seasoning at Charlotte, Wynn had a trial at Washington. He had an official record of none won, 2 lost. He won 9 and lost 7 at Charlotte in 1940. In 1941 he had a 16-won, 12-lost mark at Springfield of the Eastern League. Winding up the year at Washington, Wynn won 3 and lost one. From then on, he was a major league regular except for 1945, which he spent in military service.

Wynn's high marks at Washington were 18 won in 1943 and 17 in 1947. He lost 19, while winning only 8, in the disappointing 1948 campaign. There followed an important event in Wynn's career. On December 14, 1948, he was traded to Cleveland, along with first baseman Mickey Vernon, for pitchers Joe Haynes and Ed Klieman and first baseman Eddie Robinson. What a deal Bill Veeck had made for Cleveland!

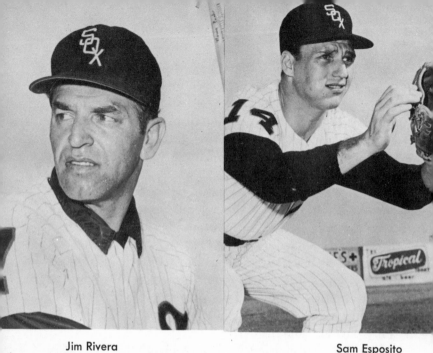

Jim Rivera

Sam Esposito

Earl Torgeson

Bob Shaw

Wynn hit his stride at Cleveland, winning 20 or more games in four of nine seasons. He said, "The biggest thing that ever happened to me in baseball was Mel Harder, Cleveland's great pitcher and pitching coach. Harder improved my curve, slider, and control. He taught me fundamentals, so I could find the trouble when my curve and slider weren't breaking. Harder made me realize that nothing concerns a pitcher except the player at bat. Unless the bases are filled, or the winning run is on, a pitcher cannot afford to be distracted from the batter."

Harder polished big Early's style, but no one had to teach him nerve. Major-leaguers saw Wynn's spunk shortly after he reported for that brief 1939 stay with the Senators. Cleveland's Ben Chapman, pausing in the Senators' clubhouse, asked Manager Bucky Harris who had drawn the Washington pitching assignment. Harris pointed to nineteen-year-old Wynn.

"I'll get five hits," said Chapman, matter-of-factly.

"If you get five hits," said Wynn, "the last three will be from a prone position."

That scored some points for Wynn. But he was thrown for a loss in another game against Cleveland. In a late inning the Senators led by a run and had two runners on base with none out. Wynn's turn to bat!

"Can you bunt?" asked Harris.

"I'm a good bunter," said Early.

"Then lay one down."

Wynn laid one down that was turned into a triple play. That night he was an ex-Senator on his way to the minors.

Tragedy hit in 1941, when his wife, Mabel, was killed in an automobile crash. The youthful pitcher was left with an infant son, Joe Early Wynn. Early married Lorraine Follin on September 12, 1944.

Early proudly watched Joe Early develop into a promising ballplayer, and in '58 he'd go out to Comiskey Park early in the morning to pitch some batting practice for young Joe. One day the kid teed off and whistled a couple of drives to the fence. Next thing Joe knew, he was sprawled flat in the dust. Early Wynn let no batter dig in on him, even if it was his own son.

Larry Doby, first Negro in the American League, knew Wynn's pitching philosophy from way back. Doby often said that at Cleveland he had enjoyed playing most on days when Wynn pitched. On those days Doby knew he was not going to be knocked down by the rival pitcher; they wouldn't dare invite Early to throw at their hitters.

Rival batters quickly tabbed Wynn as a mound monster who went by no code except survival of the fittest. Newspapermen soon learned he would speak as bluntly as Rogers Hornsby or Frank Lane. Many a day a writer raced to his typewriter with some scorching copy provided by Wynn. He is also a fine, generous fellow with a serious ambition to expand his Florida construction business, and he's something of a psychologist, with a sly sense of humor.

Take the time in spring training when Wynn had twoscore writers, radio men, and White Sox officials to dinner at his home. Lou Burdette (he signs his nickname "Lou" although it comes from Lewis) of the Braves helped him entertain and keep the glasses filled.

Came time to eat and Wynn wandered through the crowd writing down orders for barbecued steaks. Rare? Medium? Well done? The orders taken, Chef Wynn and Assistant Chef Burdette went to the charcoal grill. Soon the guests were putting away "the finest steaks ever tasted in Florida." Wynn rapped for attention. "Everyone got his steak done just right?"

There was a chorus of yeses.

"I'm glad," laughed Wynn, "because they're all cooked the same. I've never seen anybody know what he wants till he's had it."

The influence of Early Wynn was felt by the White Sox pitching corps before Early ever donned a Chicago uniform. His influence was there in the person of Richard Edward

(Dick) Donovan, a right-handed pitcher born in Quincy, Massachusetts, on December 7, 1927.

Donovan, who became an established major-leaguer in Chicago after several bleak seasons as a nomad, had Wynn as his pitching model. "I study the way Wynn works. He plays cat-and-mouse with the batter. He's the pitcher's pitcher. He goes into the game with a positive mental attitude and dominates the situation."

Purchased by the White Sox after winning 18 and losing 8 at Atlanta in 1954, tricky Dick got off to a fast start in '55, the year the Go-Go Sox *almost* won the pennant. He had won 13 and lost 4 when he was stricken with appendicitis and flown to Chicago for an emergency appendectomy. While recuperating in Mercy Hospital, Dick thought he still was jinxed by the hard luck that had followed him almost since he had stepped into Organized Baseball with Fort Lauderdale in 1947. But although he won only 2 and lost 5 after his return from sick bay, and the White Sox finished third, he was already established as a cog in the Chicago machine.

Donovan was seventeen years old and making $90 a week in the shipyards when the Boston Braves offered him $125 a month. Tricky Dick accepted it, and began a life of baseball frustration.

Part of the frustration may have been due to a volatile temper that Dick showed little sign of controlling till 1959 and his marriage to Patricia Casey, a former airline stewardess. Even mellowed by marriage, Donovan retained some unkind feelings toward the Braves.

Donovan's father had been a semi-pro baseball player and used to hit him fungoes in the days when Dick was an infielder on the Sacred Heart parish team in North Quincy, Massachusetts. Dick still was an infielder when he made the varsity as a junior at North Quincy High School, and he remained an infielder until, in his senior year, North Quincy found its pitching corps depleted on the day of its game with archrival Quincy. Coach Hal Forrest, thinking of Donovan's

Turk Lown

Sherman Lollar

Jim McAnany

Dick Donovan

strong arm, said he needed a volunteer for pitcher, then pointed at Donovan: "You're the pitcher.'"

Donovan went twelve innings to beat Quincy, 1–0.

He pitched out the season; then, certain his playing days were over, took the shipyards job. But someone stepped forward to help Dick Donovan. This first of his many benefactors was a co-worker who had a relative on the Braves' scouting staff. The relative was tipped off about Dick, and the contract with the Braves resulted. Again disappointment loomed. Uncle Sam, who would pay almost as much as the Braves, called Donovan into service.

Finally came 1947, and the chance at Fort Lauderdale. Dick issued 104 bases on balls and won only seven games. Still he impressed someone, and went on to the Evansville, Indiana, Three-I League club in 1948. There he won 12 and fanned 140, so the Braves graduated him to Milwaukee, of the American Association, for 1949.

But Jake Flowers of Milwaukee was unimpressed and shipped Donovan to Hartford of the Eastern League. Hartford offered him $325 a month. Donoven said, "I was making $450 at Milwaukee. I'll go home before I'll sign that contract."

Hartford said to sign, or else. Donovan went home to Quincy, but eventually reconsidered and joined Hartford. There he won 12.

Dick started with Boston in 1950 and lost 2. Back to Milwaukee, where he won 3 and lost 6. The next two seasons it was the same story: briefly with the Braves, then a windup with Milwaukee. By the end of 1952, pitcher Dick Donovan had appeared in twenty-five major league games — and lost all four decisions!

Things looked better in 1953, when Donovan again found himself ticketed for Milwaukee — because now Milwaukee was the home of the major league Braves. The bubble burst the instant Milwaukee told Donovan he had been sold to their Toledo club. Donovan was furious.

Along the way Donovan had a flare-up with John Quinn,

then general manager of the Braves, and demanded a release from the organization. Quinn said the Braves were obliged to protect their investment.

"What investment?" snarled Donovan. "All it cost to sign me was thirty cents carfare — and I paid that myself."

Finally Donovan received the Braves' permission to work out a deal for himself; all they asked was a player in return. He tried many clubs, including the White Sox, but General Manager Frank Lane had scouting reports that did not rate Donovan high. As rejection followed repection, Donovan brooded more. His big-league career was only a dream, after all.

This time his benefactor was Gene Mauch, a former team-mate now managing Atlanta of the Southern Association. Mauch wanted Donovan; somewhat reluctantly, Donovan went to Atlanta. What had convinced him to give baseball another chance was a casual train conversation with Whitlow Wyatt, the former major league pitcher who was coaching for Mauch. Sitting beside Donovan en route to New Orleans, Wyatt said, "I'm amazed that Bucky Walters never won his first big-league game until he was twenty-seven, and then won 198.

"Look at the case of Dazzy Vance. He won 198 after he was thirty-one. And look at me. I kicked around for a long time, in the minors and majors. I was almost thirty and ready to quit when Milwaukee persuaded me to come to spring training. That season I started fooling around with a slow curve, mixing it with my fast ball. So I won twenty-four games for Milwaukee and was sold to Brooklyn for $40,000. The year I was thirty-four I won twenty-two for the Dodgers."

That was exactly the pep talk Donovan needed. He stayed with Atlanta, winning 11 and losing 8. Spring of 1954 found him up with Detroit. The Tigers, who had practically made the White Sox a gift of Billy Pierce, and who were later to make the mistake of letting the Sox get Bob Shaw, did Chicago another favor. They shunted Donovan back to Atlanta, where he found that Wyatt had replaced Mauch as manager. Determined to prove the Braves and everyone else made a mistake, encouraged and urged on by Whitlow Wyatt, in 1954 Dick Donovan won 18 games and attracted the attention of the White Sox. This time Frank Lane disregarded his scouts' reports and set out to snare the young man.

When Donovan reported to the White Sox in 1955, he brought along something new — the slider Wyatt had taught him. It had taken Dick a half hour to master the pitch and all season to mix it up properly with his fast ball and curve.

The slider was to make Donovan a winner, although there were doubts in Manager Marion's mind as Donovan made his first White Sox start. The Athletics were making merry at pitcher Donovan's expense.

As Dick saw Marion stride out to relieve him, tears welled in his eyes. After all these years, he was to fail again. No, he wouldn't! Donovan refused to yield the ball.

Marion said, "Come on, Dick, it's one of those things. You'll be our starter when your regular turn comes up again."

Donovan trudged away disconsolate. That evening he was brooding in the hotel when catcher Sherman Lollar invited him to his room. As Donovan later recalled: "Sherman opened a few cans of beer, and talked just like I was a White Sox regular. Later in the evening, feeling better, I bumped into Frank Lane. He said that I'd get my regular start, as Marion promised, and that no matter what happened, I was with the White Sox to stay."

The long trail of detours had ended. The path ahead seemed smooth, particularly after Dick blanked the Red Sox on five hits the next time out.

Dick Donovan was to become one of the Go-Go regulars, and with his future assured, he forgot past disappointments. He even could joke, and except on pitching day, he was so good-humored that no one was surprised at his answer when a young tyke asked him, "Suppose you were pitching against the Yankees and Mickey Mantle came to bat with the bases filled. What would you do?"

Said Dick, "I'd look around to see who the manager was bringing in as the relief pitcher."

The encouragement and helping hand given Donovan by Sox catcher Sherman Lollar has gone to many another of the Go-Go White Sox. For catcher John Sherman Lollar was the Gibraltar of the Go-Go White Sox, on and off the field, in good times and bad. Sherman is not only an exceptionally dependable backstop, he also led the White Sox in homers in 1958 and 1959.

The baseball career of Sherman Lollar, born August 23, 1924, in Durham, Arkansas, has been more varied than one would suspect. Lollar was involved in the most controversial play of the 1959 World Series. He also was behind the plate the day Babe Ruth hit his historic No. 60 homer — at least Lollar was the catcher in the movie version of Babe Ruth's life. And Lollar's career was otherwise a surprising one.

One morning in the lobby of Miami's Biscayne Terrace Lollar told me, "I was a kid of nineteen, and never had earned more than eighteen dollars a week, when I was offered thirty-seven dollars a week to work in a lead mine at Baxter Springs, Kansas. With the job came the chance to play with Barney Barnett's company baseball team. I accepted the job, and the baseball chance. It seemed a wonderful break. You see, my father, who operated a grocery store in Fayetteville, Arkansas, had died when I was a little boy. My mother worked as a librarian to support us. I graduated from high school in Fayetteville, then went to Pittsburg, Kansas, to attend Pittsburg State Teachers College. I was attending college and making maybe thirteen dollars a week when the offer came from Baxter Springs.

"While catching at Baxter Springs, I met a miner named Stan West, who was in an essential war industry. Stan also belonged to the Baltimore Orioles and recommended me to Tommy Thomas, a former White Sox pitcher, who managed

the Orioles, then in the International League. I got to Baltimore, in time to play twelve games in 1943, and I hit .118."

Lollar hit .250 at Baltimore in 1944, then zoomed to .364 in
1945. The healthy batting average earned him a shot with
Cleveland in 1946. Cleveland manager Lou Boudreau was not
impressed; he thought Lollar lacked aggressiveness, had no
take-charge spirit. More impressive, in Boudreau's eyes, was a
young catcher named Jim Hegan, just returned from military
service. So Boudreau concluded that young Lollar would sit
on the bench. Lollar thought otherwise, and voiced his opinion
to Boudreau.

"Are you nuts?" said Boudreau. "Kids work years to get a
chance in the majors, and you want to be sent back down.
Don't you know that the second chance may never come?"

Lollar said he didn't care; if he could not play in Cleveland
every day, he wanted to go back to Baltimore. His wish was
granted, and he delighted no one in Baltimore by hitting .234.
Cleveland figured it had best trade Lollar while he was still
worth something; so he went to the Yankees, with infielder
Ray Mack, for pitchers Al Gettel and Gene Bearden and
outfielder Hal Peck. The man who made the swap from the
Cleveland end was young Bill Veeck.

At New York, Lollar joined such catchers as Gus Niarhos,
Charley Silvera, Aaron Robinson, and young Yogi Berra. The
Yanks sent him to Newark for 111 games, but he was back in
time to catch two of their 1947 World Series matches with
Brooklyn. The 1948 season was spent entirely with the
Yankees, and almost entirely on the bench. In December of
1948, Lollar was part of a Yankee Christmas present sent to
the St. Louis Browns. With him went pitchers Red Embree
and Dick Starr and $100,000 folding money. The Browns sent
the Yankees pitcher Fred Sanford and catcher Roy Partee.

At least Lollar played in St. Louis — 333 games in three
seasons. Following the 1951 season, General Manager Lane of
Chicago and Boss Bill Veeck, now of the Browns, let their
imaginations run wild. When the countdown came, an eight-

player swap had been consummated and Lollar was fitting on a Chicago uniform. Lane said, at the time, "Paul Richards figured that Lollar would be a key player in our plans to build a pennant winner in Chicago. So did I."

Lollar was a key player, although the pennant was a long time in coming.

Richards afterwards was not certain that Chicago had struck a great bargain in obtaining Lollar. Though Lollar saw action in more than 100 games in each of his years under Richards, he was often chagrined at being platooned with Phil Masi, Matt Batts, Carl Sawatski, Bud Sheely, and others. Lollar's big break came when Marty Marion was named manager to succeed Richards. Marion told him, "You're to be our regular catcher."

Lollar was, too, despite the challenge of Clint Courtney, who in 1955 checked in with the cocky announcement: "I'm going to be your first-string catcher." Before the season was very old, Courtney was on his way to join the Senators.

General Sherman, besides being a steadying force on the field, became a leader in the clubhouse. For example, when he learned that the White Sox bat boy was graduating from high school, Lollar circulated among his teammates to collect money for a wrist watch.

Lollar's sense of humor is wry and quiet, but memorable. One afternoon in a scoreless contest the Yankees filled the bases with none out; and Mickey Mantle, Yogi Berra, and Johnny Mize were coming to bat. Lollar started from the plate to huddle with pitcher Sandy Consuegra, who spoke no English. But Nellie Fox and Chico Carrasquel, the team interpreter, beat him to the mound. Whereupon Umpire Bill McGowan said, "You can't go out, Sherman. The rules say no more than two players can talk with the pitcher."

Lollar handed the ball to McGowan and drawled, "That's dandy, Bill. You just go out and tell Consuegra how he should pitch to Mantle and Berra."

Sherman Lollar, Early Wynn, Dick Donovan, Lu Aparicio, Nellie Fox, Jim Landis, Billy Pierce — these were established White Sox stars on hand as Manager Al Lopez called his first roll of the 1959 training season. But there were other possibilities — outfielders Jim Rivera and Al Smith, and that kid pitcher from Detroit, Bob Shaw.

Rivera, who had come to Chicago from the Browns in 1952, hit .255 in 1956, .256 in 1957, and .225 in 1958. Lopez had told him after the '58 campaign, "Jim, with your head-first slides and everything, you're the most exciting player in baseball once you get on base. The only trouble is getting you on base. If you would improve your hitting, you could earn thirty thousand a year even at your age."

Rivera's age was not the question; although the record books reported he was born on July 22, 1923, Jim freely admits to having checked in two years earlier. Even at thirty-seven this spring of 1959, he was still the most picturesque of the White Sox, and had been a defensive mainstay since his arrival. And one season during the formative years of the Go-Go White Sox, Jim had actually led the club in homers.

Chuck Comiskey, of all the White Sox family, was the most dedicated Rivera fan. He had kept Jungle Jim in baseball after certain allegations were made against him, and he demonstrated his confidence by offering Jim a contract for the following year. Amazed at the speed with which Jim signed, Chuck asked, "Don't you even want to read what it says?"

"Why read it?" said Rivera. "Where else can I go if I don't like it here?"

Each payday Chuck deducted a goodly amount from Jim's salary and banked it for him. After the season, Jim wanted to buy a new car. Chuck was in agreement until he learned that Rivera planned to pay cash for a dolled-up Cadillac and needed more than $7,000. The exact price was only $200 less than Rivera had saved. Comiskey handed him a check for the entire savings.

"But you gave me the extra two hundred dollars," Rivera said.

"I know," said Comiskey. "You might want to leave a tip someplace."

It was Jim's automobile that prompted Frank Lane to snap, "This league has too many .250 hitters driving Cadillacs."

Lane was often exasperated by Rivera. Frequently Jim, failing to make a play exactly as Lane thought it should have been made, would draw Frank's favorite barb: "I didn't know they allowed spectators on the field." There were other times, though, when Lane was absolutely delighted by Rivera. He never tired of telling of an incident that followed a Sox night victory in Kansas City.

After dressing, Rivera left the park with George Kell. Outside, Kell spotted former President Harry Truman. Said Kell, "I'd like to introduce myself, Mr. Truman, and this is Jim Rivera, who hit the winning home run."

"Let me call my wife over," said Mr. Truman. "She's the real fan. Bess, this is the man who hit the home run."

Through clouds of cigar smoke, Jungle Jim critically eyed Mr. and Mrs. Harry Truman. Then he said, "Hiyah, Bess. Sorry we had to hang one on you."

Alphonse E. (Al) Smith reported in 1959 as a question mark. White Sox hopes had been high when Smith, born February 7, 1928, in Kirkwood, Missouri, came to the club with Wynn in the Minoso-Hatfield swap. There was disappointment the year before when Al hit only .252 and batted in only 58 runs. The White Sox fans had gotten on him, few realizing that Al was playing without complaint despite a painful leg.

Smith had broken into Organized Baseball in 1948 with Wilkes-Barre, hitting .316. Though he had been regarded as one of the finest high school players in Missouri history, once running for ten touchdowns in a single football game, Smith had turned down an offer from the Cleveland Browns and had bet his future on baseball. By 1953 it was apparent he had made the right bet, because late that year, after moving from Wilkes-Barre to San Diego to Indianapolis, he won a regular's post at Cleveland. In 1955 he hit twenty-two homers. Soon came the trade to Chicago, and a mediocre year.

Would 1959 be another step down for Al Smith? Or would he come back? Al Lopez was an incurable optimist, but even he did not foresee the game-smashing homers that Smith was to deliver during the greatest Go-Go year.

Handsome Bob Shaw, born in Garden City, New York, on June 29, 1933, caused little stir at this early moment in pre-season preparations. Even newspapermen hard pressed for mail features seldom bothered him; and it was not until Bob established himself as starter midway in the championship campaign that I cornered him at a party at Patsy Trella's. He told me his story:

"I passed up my first chance to sign with a big-league club because I wanted to play football at St. Lawrence College. But my sophomore year I had to sleep on a dormitory floor, and the snow would blow in at night and melt against the radiator, flooding my bed. So I forgot football and took a thousand dollars to sign with the Tigers.

"I made the usual stops — Jamestown, Durham, Augusta, Syracuse, Toronto, and Charleston, before finally getting a chance at Detroit.

"Early in 1958 I was in trouble with the Tigers — money troubles and few chances to pitch. I refused to be shipped to Charleston because I knew I could pitch big-league ball. So on June 15, Detroit sent me and Ike Boone to Chicago for Bill Fischer and Tito Francona. It was my greatest break.

"I won four in a row in relief after joining Chicago. I was with good teachers. Manager Lopez had confidence in me; and then there were Coach Ray Berres and Dick Donovan to advise me. I began throwing my slider the way Donovan threw his. Last winter, in Cuba, I worked on fundamentals. At Lopez's suggestion, I began pitching completely overhand, instead of sidearm and three-quarter."

Billy Goodman

Ray Moore

So, in 1959, the 195-pound right-hander came fast — so fast that late in the season owner Veeck shuddered each time he remembered his attempts to peddle Shaw to Cleveland early in the season. The Go-Go White Sox might not have gone if Shaw hadn't blossomed to take up the slack left by Donovan and Pierce.

Of course there were more than stars like Fox and Wynn and Aparicio, more than stars-to-be like Bob Shaw, and more than promising rookies like Barry Latman and John Callison and Jim McAnany, on hand when the Go-Go White Sox assembled in Tampa to lay battle plans for 1959. There were those standing aside from the stars and apart from the promising rookies. They were the hard corps of journeyman ball-players and the troop of youngsters hopeful of not being sent back to the farms for additional seasons. They included:

Infielder Billy Goodman, born March 22, 1926, in Concord, North Carolina. Goodman had been only eighteen when he accepted a $1,200 bonus from the Atlanta Crackers. He was an established major-leaguer with the Red Sox from 1948 until mid-1957, when he was swapped to Baltimore. Then the Orioles shipped him, along with Tito Francona and Ray Moore, to Chicago in exchange for Larry Doby, Jack Harshman, Jim Marshall, and Russ Heman, in December, 1957. Goodman had hit .299 in his first season with the White Sox.

Infielder John (Bubba) Phillips, born February 24, 1930, in West Point, Mississippi.

First baseman Earl Torgeson, an old pro born January 1, 1924, in Snohomish, Washington, and a 1948 World Series participant as a member of the Boston Braves. Earl's baseball career had included stops at Wenatchee (when he was seventeen), Seattle, Spokane, Boston, the Phillies, and the Tigers, who traded him to Chicago for outfielder-infielder Dave Philley on June 13, 1957.

First baseman Ray Boone, born July 27, 1923, in San Diego, California. An Indian and a Tiger before joining the White Sox, a catcher when he broke in at Wausau in 1942, Boone had been changed to third base, and then to first base. In 1953 he had hit four grand-slam homers.

First baseman Ron Jackson, born October 22, 1933, in Kalamazoo — a six-foot, seven-inch bonus boy from Western Michigan College.

Catcher Earl Battey, born January 8, 1935; Three-I League rookie of the year in 1954, with one full White Sox season already behind him. A good catcher but weak hitter, Battey was acquired from Charleston in September of 1954 in exchange for pitcher Vito Valentinetti.

Catcher John Romano, born August 23, 1934, in Hoboken, New Jersey.

Catcher Charles (Chuck) Lindstrom, born in Chicago, Illinois, on September 7, 1936. A former star at Northwestern University and once voted the outstanding player in the American Legion national tournament, Chuck came in with a great heritage — his father was the same Fred Lindstrom who had been John J. McGraw's New York Giant. No one, of course, expected Lindstrom to go great with the White Sox in 1959. He didn't.

Catcher Les Moss, born May 14, 1925, in Tulsa, Oklahoma; a respected veteran who had played in St. Louis, Boston, and Baltimore, before being traded to Chicago for pitcher Harry Dorish in June, 1955. With Battey on hand in 1958, Moss had been in only two games and was at bat only once, yet in 1956 he had hit twenty-two homers for the White Sox.

Infielder Sam Esposito, a home-town favorite, born December 15, 1931. In mid-season, the White Sox would ask waivers on the scrappy little man, and six clubs would claim him! The waivers would be withdrawn.

Outfielder Lou Skizas, once a potential Yankee, born on July 2, 1931, in Berwyn, a Chicago suburb. A draft choice in 1958, Skizas was to have an inspection, but was not to stay.

Jim McAnany, of course — born September 4, 1938, and signed by Hollis (Sloppy) Thurston after a freshman year at the University of Southern California. Purchased from Colorado Springs in 1958, after hitting .400 there, Jim was destined for a more important role than seemed likely when he first reported to spring training in '59.

Outfielder Don Mueller, born April 14, 1927, in St. Louis, Missouri. Don had been purchased from the San Francisco Giants in 1958 but was not destined to remain with the Go-Go Sox in '59.

Outfielder Norman Cash, born November 10, 1934, at Justiceburg, Texas, and one-time football star at tiny Sul Ross College in Alpine, Texas. Norm signed as a free agent on May 20, 1955; military service followed his apprenticeship at Waterloo. 1958 he divided between Chicago and Indianapolis, where he played in a combined total of only forty-two games. Since then good reports had come in on Cash's play in the winter league.

Outfielder Joe Hicks, born April 7, 1933, at Ivy, Virginia; a .381 hitter at Colorado Springs in 1958.

Pitcher Omar (Turk) Lown, born May 30, 1924, purchased from Cincinnati on June 23, 1958. This right-hander, who had learned his craft with the Chicago Cubs, was to play a major role in relief.

Pitcher Gerald Staley, born August 21, 1921, in Brush Prairie, Washington. A right-hander who, like Lown, had learned the trade in the National League (Cardinals), Gerry had been purchased from the Yankees in late May, 1956. He was to become the absolute ace of the relief corps.

Pitcher Claude Raymond, right-hander born May 7, 1937, at St. Jean, Quebec, Canada.

Pitcher Ray Moore, right-hander born June 1, 1926, in Upper Marlboro, Maryland. Ray's debut in Organized Baseball came back in 1947, with the Dodger organization. He reached Chicago in the big swap with Baltimore in December, 1957, and won nine, while losing seven, for the 1958 club.

Pitcher Rodolfo Arias, born June 6, 1931, in De Oriente, Cuba. Along with Joe Hicks, Arias was acquired from Indianapolis after the 1958 season in exchange for Dick Di Tusa and Ted Beard. As a lefty Arias had an edge and was to remain with the White Sox through the championship season and World Series.

Pitcher Stover McIlwain, a right-hander born September 22, 1939, in Savannah, Georgia. He pitched at Rollins College, was signed by Zack Taylor in 1957.

Pitcher Bill Du Four, born December 14, 1930, in Wyandotte, Michigan. Bill was a right-hander making his fourth appearance at a White Sox spring training base.

Pitcher Tom Qualters, born April 1, 1935, in Allison Park, Pennsylvania, and signed to a Phillies bonus contract in 1953. The White Sox purchased Tom from Philadelphia on April 30, 1958; through the season he was to pitch forty-four innings without decision.

Left-hander Don Rudolph, born August 16, 1931, in Baltimore, Maryland. Don had been purchased from Memphis on October 16, 1956, and had made brief appearances (nineteen innings) on the mound for the Sox in 1957 and 1958. Many were pulling for Don; he received almost as much publicity as his wife, a professional dancer named Patti Waggin.

Pitcher Hal Trosky, a right-hander born September 29, 1936, the son of famous former White Sox first baseman Hal Trosky.

Those were the Go-Go White Sox in camp when the roll was called in the spring of 1959. Some were to go great guns. Others were to go. And some were to come, including the veterans Larry Doby and Del Ennis and Harry (Suitcase) Simpson.

Best of all, when the pennant express was moving full speed ahead, Ted Kluszewski was to come.

CHAPTER 12

How They Won It in '59

THE 1959 Go-Go Chicago White Sox wasted no time in getting on the trail that led to rainbow's end in Cleveland on September 22. They started on opening day as Nellie Fox laced out a fourteenth-inning homer, with Sammy Esposito on base, to whip the Tigers, 9–7, before 38,332 chilled spectators in Detroit. The decision went to Gerry Staley, one of seven Chicago pitchers to find employment that afternoon. The four hour and twenty-five minute marathon was concluded by Fox's first major league homer since September 19, 1957, when Washington's Pedro Ramos had been victimized.

Next afternoon, Ol' Early Wynn signaled the beginning of a great year for himself. He checked the Tigers with seven hits, won, 5–3, on two home runs by Sherman Lollar and one by Luis Aparicio. It was the two hundred and fiftieth victory of his big-league career.

On Tuesday, April 14, the White Sox made their home debut with the Kansas City Athletics as the opposition and the Chicago favorite, Billy Pierce, on the mound. The game received wide advance publicity, and everyone wondered what stunts Veeck might unveil in his home-town debut as

White Sox impresario. He had tried to produce Fidel Castro and failed, and his fireworks display fizzled; but the fans appreciated his invitation to grab free beer and soda, and Billy Pierce's six-hit, 2–0 shutout sent them home happy.

Veeck himself went home disappointed. He had secretly told some of his backers he hoped to draw 1,200,000 for the year, and the opening-day crowd of 19,303 had not been encouraging. On the credit side was the fact that the Sox had now won three in a row without a loss.

On April 17 Jim Rivera drove in two runs with an eighth-inning double to pace a 6–5 victory over the Athletics, and terminate a two-game losing streak. The Athletics again were the principals on April 22, in Kansas City, and the game was one of the season's most comical. Chicago scored 11 runs in the seventh inning on one hit, 10 walks, a hit batsman, and an error, to edge out the A's, 20–6.

Earl Torgeson got a three-run pinch homer in the ninth to beat Cleveland, 8–6, on April 25. Next day Cleveland absorbed a twin whipping, 6–5 and 5–2.

Al Smith's eleventh-inning single drove in the run that beat the Yankees, 4–3, on April 30, Pierce getting the decision. Wynn provided all the heroics on the first day of May; he pitched a one-hitter and walloped an eighth-inning homer for a 1–0 conquest of the Red Sox.

A May 9 defeat of Cleveland, 9–5, ended a five-game losing streak. A double loss was dealt the Indians the following afternoon. Billy Goodman and Bubba Phillips drove in the tying and winning runs in the 5–4, eleven-inning opener. Wynn baffled the Indians on four hits in the 5–0 afterpiece.

On May 12 in Boston, Nellie Fox's sixteen-game consecutive hitting streak came to an end, but the White Sox won, 4–3, on Al Smith's twelfth-inning home run.

The next game was one that Bob Shaw never will forget. It was his first starting assignment of the year, and he produced a five-hit, 4–0 victory over the Red Sox.

Billy Pierce blanked the Yankees, 6–0, on six hits, on May

This time Little Luis didn't arrive safely.

15. On May 16, Chicago ran its winning streak to eight in a row as Del Ennis drove in an eleventh-inning run to conquer the Yankees, 4–3. Pitcher Pedro Ramos of the Senators then ended the winning streak, 4–2, in the opener of a Washington doubleheader. The White Sox rebounded in the second game, 10–7, and the next day beat the Nats again, 9–2. This victory, their tenth in eleven games, shot the White Sox into the league lead for the first time since June 25, 1957. The winning pitcher? Wynn himself.

The first-place tenancy lasted only until the following evening, as pitcher Billy O'Dell's homer scored both Baltimore runs in a 2–1 win over Billy Pierce. Cleveland, meanwhile, went into the top spot with a victory over Washington.

One of the Go-Go gang's patented "cliff-hanger" decisions went into the scorebooks in Kansas City the night of May 22. Chicago held a 2–1 lead when the Athletics came up in the ninth, and Bob Shaw was working on a three-hitter. With one out, Jim Rivera dropped a soft fly off the bat of Hector Lopez. After Hector was forced out by Preston Ward, Frank House singled and pinch hitter Kent Hadley drew a walk, filling the bases and inspiring Al Lopez to summon Turk Lown.

Kansas City sent up Dick Williams to bat for pitcher Bob Grim. Williams whipped out a sinking line drive, a hit against almost any center fielder except the White Sox antelope, Jim Landis. Jim made a diving catch to preserve the 2–1 edge.

Earl Torgeson and Sherman Lollar hit home runs in the 5–1 victory over Cleveland, on May 27, to get Chicago back on the victory path following a three-game losing streak.

Detroit was a 4–3 victim on May 30. Nellie Fox and John (Honey) Romano drove in ninth-inning runs.

June 4 dawned with the White Sox in a first-place tie with Cleveland. It ended with Chicago one-half game ahead. The lead was gained the hard way, in seventeen innings. Earl Torgeson's home run sealed the 6–5 conquest.

Early Wynn pitched a five-hitter, and Lu Aparicio stole his seventeenth and eighteenth bases of the season, in the 4–1 victory over Washington on June 10. Next day Washington fell, 3–1, to Pierce's one-hitter. Landis broke a 1–1 ninth-inning deadlock with a double.

On June 14, Al Smith drove in the winning run in the tenth, the Orioles succumbing by a 3–2 score to Dick Donovan.

In the first game against Boston on June 21, the White Sox suffered a fifth consecutive defeat and were in fifth place. Billy Pierce rallied his mates by winning the second-game doubleheader, 3–2.

Harry (Suitcase) Simpson, a veteran who was destined for only a brief stay in White Sox uniform, poled a grand-slam homer to beat New York, 5–4, in Comiskey Park on June 27.

The next day Chicagoans were treated to 9–2 and 4–2 victories over the Yankees, courtesy of Early Wynn and Dick Donovan. There were home runs by Sherman Lollar (2), Earl Battey, Al Smith, and Bubba Phillips. For an added treat Promoter Veeck assembled ten elephants, bareback riders, a sword swallower, snake charmer, clowns, and — you guessed it, midgets! All that, and a double defeat of the Yankees!

Cleveland was a 6–5 victim on July 1. Lu Aparicio walked in the ninth, stole second, advanced to third on an infield hit, and scampered in with the winning run on a sacrifice.

Al Smith's grand-slam homer in Detroit the night of July 2 went for nothing as the White Sox fell, 9–7. He hit another homer the following day, a tenth-inning smash giving Chicago a 6–5 win.

Honey Romano, Bubba Phillips, and Sherman Lollar got into the home run act in Kansas City on Saturday, July 4, as the White Sox salvaged half of the doubleheader, 7–4. On Sunday Lu Aparicio, who had singled and stolen second, scored the winning run in the tenth on Nellie Fox's single.

Cleveland was beaten, 4–3, in a night game in Chicago following the All-Star game layoff. The Indians retaliated with an 8–4 defeat of the Chicagoans. Then Chicago touched off a five-game winning streak, the fifth coming in the opener of a doubleheader in Boston, 4–3, on a combination four-hitter by

Dick Donovan and Gerry Staley. Boston ruined the streak, 5–4, in the second game.

At New York, on the night of July 17, Early Wynn and Ralph Terry hooked up in a duel of two-hitters. Jim Landis drove in the runs in the ninth to win, 2–0. Gerry Staley made one pitch the following afternoon, forcing a double play, to preserve a 2–1 win for Bob Shaw.

The White Sox escaped home after losing a Sunday doubleheader in New York, and on Tuesday posted a 2–1 conquest of Boston behind Dick Donovan. A few glorious days followed. On Wednesday, July 22, Sherman Lollar batted in a ninth-inning run for a 5–4 victory. Baltimore came to town on July 24, and Al Smith's ninth-inning homer defeated the Orioles and Hoyt Wilhelm, 2–1. Suitcase Simpson was the next afternoon's hero, getting a seventh-inning pinch single off Billy Loes with the bases loaded for the 3–2 triumph that preserved a half-game lead over Cleveland's tenacious Indians. There was an even split in the Sunday doubleheader as Wynn set down the Orioles in the opener, 4–1, on a two-hitter.

Cleveland and Chicago were tied for the lead on July 28, which found Chicago entertaining New York and Cleveland playing a twilight-night doubleheader against Boston. Cleveland divided its doubleheader, and Chicago surged to the top as Billy Pierce stopped the Yankees, 4–3, on Al Smith's two-run, eighth-inning homer.

Rain broke up the game on July 29, with the score at 4–4. The Yanks fled town after falling to Wynn's six-hitter, 3–1, on July 30. The next evening was a big one for Barry Latman, who shackled the Senators with four hits, 7–1. Ray Moore and Gerry Staley checked the Senators, 2–1, on August 1, and Washington was whacked with a double loss on the following Sunday.

An eastern trip followed, and the first highlight was Barry Latman's 2–0, three-hit victory over Baltimore on August 5. There was an eighteen-inning, 1–1 tie the next day, and Chicago headed to Washington with a one and one-half game lead. The White Sox left Washington with a two and one-half game lead, Wynn's three-hit, 9–0 Sunday success being the feature of the series.

Wynn pitched another three-hit, 9–0 victory, his sixteenth of the season, and the White Sox hit four homers, at Detroit on August 13. In Kansas City the following night Sherman Lollar hit two homers and Bob Shaw turned in a 5–1 five-hitter. And the White Sox led by four games!

The lead was four and one-half games after a 6–4 lacing of Baltimore on August 18. Baltimore won the next two before Washington succumbed, 5–4, on Friday night. That Friday evening Nellie Fox was showered with gifts by the committee headed by Harry Kipke, former University of Michigan football coach.

Barry Latman's five-hitter blanked Washington, 1–0, on Saturday.

A crowd of 44,520, largest Comiskey Park daytime gathering of the campaign, was on hand for Sunday's doubleheader with the Yankees. New York took the opener, then yielded to Bob Shaw's nifty six-hit pitching, 5–0. On Monday, in the replay of the 4–4 tie of July 29, the Sox slapped the Yanks, 4–2, behind Ray Moore and Turk Lown.

The Sox were idle Tuesday, but there was big news. Suitcase Simpson was to depart the club, and the White Sox had gotten Ted Kluszewski, erstwhile National League home run king!

The White Sox held a one and one-half game lead the following Friday when they invaded Cleveland for a four-game showdown. A crowd of 70,398 was on hand for the night opener. Most left in disappointment. Sparked by Bob Shaw's pitching and Sherman Lollar's three-run homer, the Sox won, 7–3.

On Saturday afternoon, August 29, after Ken McBride, the announced starter, came down with tonsilitis, Tricky Dick Donovan produced one of his typical clutch performances, handcuffing the Indians with five hits. The 2–0 win boosted the Sox lead to three and one-half games.

And the Indians were in for a pair of scalpings on Sunday. Early Wynn hit a home run and with Staley's help won the opener, 6–3. Barry Latman and Turk Lown pitched the second game, Al Smith driving in three runs on a homer and single. Chicago shot five and one-half games ahead.

A new seasonal attendance record, 45,410, was set the following Friday night as Cleveland checked in. When the game was over, the White Sox had a 3–2 victory, a six and one-half game lead, and Wynn his eighteenth pitching triumph of the year. But the Indians whipped the White Sox in the final two games of that series.

Still, the gap was too great.

Wynn's twentieth victory came September 12, in Baltimore, 6–1. Number 22 was posted against Detroit on September 26. But between Ol' Early's twentieth victory and his twenty-second came that big Number 21 — the pennant-clincher pitched in Cleveland on September 22!

CHAPTER 13

The World Series

SUDDENLY IT WAS SPRING. No, not really spring. Actually it was a wonderful Indian summer day — the final day of September, 1959.

But spring was in the hearts of Chicago White Sox fans. Their darlings were on the eve of Chicago's first American League World Series since 1919. After four decades of penance and frustration, Chicago's South Side once more would be host to the biggest show in baseball. In fact, some of the older settlers in Bridgeport, and Canaryville, in back of the Yards, and in far south Marynook, said that with the White Sox in it, the World Series had to be a bigger "shew" than Ed Sullivan's.

On September 30, the weatherman predicted that the great day of Thursday, October 1, would be crisp and cool. Connie Lopez, wife of the Chicago manager, predicted that the Go-Go Sox would triumph over the Los Angeles Dodgers — her heroes in the days when she and the Dodgers both were Brooklyn inhabitants — in five or six games. Lou Perini, whose Milwaukee Braves had represented the National League in the World Series of 1957 and of 1958, complained that he could not obtain extra tickets from Bill Veeck. Sport Shirt

Red Faber lets go with his famed spitter as Ray Schalk again catches his old teammate in a touching scene before

Bill said tough luck — that when he was out of baseball and needed World Series tickets to Milwaukee's County Stadium, Perini looked the other way.

Thousands wrote letters to politicians, long-forgotten friends, and Veeck. A scalper asked $125 for a choice box for the opener. Some of the White Sox official family were still red-faced because the name of a Chicago Cub fan had been first drawn in Veeck's lottery to assure more even distribution of the prized ducats. Small-time hoodlums were counterfeiting the tickets.

Jack Brickhouse of Chicago's WGN-TV and Vince Scully of Los Angeles were ready to do the telecast. Mel Allen of New York and Byrum Saam of Philadelphia were primed for the broadcast. Sports writers trouped in from all points and six countries. The New York delegation included Jimmy Cannon, Arthur Daley, Red Smith, Frank Graham, Milton Gross, Joe King, Dick Young, Dan Parker, Jimmy Powers, Dan Daniel, John Drebinger, Tommy Holmes, Harold Rosenthal. From Los Angeles came Paul Zimmerman, Braven Dyer, Mel Durslag, John B. Old, Frank Finch, Vincent X. Flaherty, and perhaps a dozen more.

Another famous writer checked into headquarters at the La Salle Hotel. He was a gnomelike, keen-eyed, impish fellow named Charles Dillon Stengel — the same Casey Stengel whose New York Yankees had been co-stars of nine previous showdowns in ten years.

Bill Veeck, in his freshman season as president of the White Sox, was entertaining in a style that would have done credit to the Old Roman, and his festive headquarters — the La Salle Hotel's grand ballroom — was packed so tight with celebrities that one wag remarked, "I'll bet Veeck would like to see a crowd like this in Comiskey Park."

Thousands were standing in the ticket lines at the venerable, spruced-up ball park on Thirty-fifth Street. Andy Frain, the famed chief usher, and police captains Joseph

Graney and John L. Sullivan were huddling on final plans to handle the crowds.

Mayor Daley, as nervous as the Chicago athletes, had seen that a special traffic plan was put into effect. This was in command of Chief Philip McGuire, veteran South Sider who had lived and died with the White Sox through the past forty years. As an added touch, the Mayor arranged blue-ribbon police escorts for buses transporting the writers to the ball park. Chicago was doing it up big.

White Sox manager Al Lopez had named ancient Early Wynn, top pitcher in the majors with twenty-two wins, to hurl the opener. Los Angeles manager Walter Alston had chosen Roger Craig, a thirty-one-year-old right-hander who had returned from minor league oblivion to be the Dodgers' leading pitcher for the final half of the campaign. And in the wee hours of October 1, as the last of the guests left the La Salle ballroom and Bill Veeck shut off his telephones to get some rest, weary-eyed Western Union operators punched out the last of the advance stories, including those of Jackie Robinson, erstwhile Dodger World Series hero, and little Dickie Kerr, a game and honest White Sox pitcher in the 1919 Series, now writing for a Houston newspaper.

October 1, 1959. Comiskey Park, the cynosure of the sports world. A crowd of 48,013, plus hundreds and hundreds of reporters, broadcasters, photographers, policemen, and ushers, were on hand. For some 20,000 women there were red roses, another Veeck touch. Jump Jackson's band, and others, were early arrivals. The traditional red-white-and-blue World Series bunting was conspicuously absent, and owner Veeck explained, "We're proud of our clean park and want fans to see it just the way it is for league play."

Manager Lopez suppressed a yawn while watching the Dodgers take batting practice. He had been awakened at 7 A.M., when Mrs. Lopez received a call from her hairdresser. Noting that Urban Faber and Ray Schalk, stars in Chicago's drive to the 1917 American League championship, were to form the battery for the opening pitch, Al remarked, "I wish they were in shape. I'd leave 'em in for the whole game."

Equipment manager Eph (Sharkey) Colledge, a veteran of more than a half century on the White Sox scene, gave a last-minute pep talk to Early Wynn: "Okay, I've been waiting for a cut of this World Series pie longer than any of you guys."

Tony Martin sang "The Star-Spangled Banner." A color guard had trouble raising Old Glory on the center field flagpole, and festivities began with the flag at half-staff. Umpire Bill Summers crouched behind catcher Cracker Schalk; pitcher Red Faber loaded up a "spitter" and delivered. "Stre-e-e-e-e-k!" Summers bellowed. And now it was time for the principals, the Go-Go White Sox and the daring Dodgers, to take over.

The Sox trotted to their positions: Sherman Lollar (.266), still cautious with his injured hand, behind the plate; Wynn on the mound; Big Klu (.297) guarding first base; Nellie Fox (.306) at second; Little Looey (.257) at short; veteran Billy Goodman (.248) at third; Jim Rivera (.226), in right field; ball-hawking Jim Landis (.272) in center; and Al Smith (.237), who had vindicated himself with White Sox fans, in left.

The Dodgers' Junior Gilliam, brandishing his war club, advanced on the plate. Wynn was taking Lollar's signal. The tension was electric. It was time to play ball!

Wynn's first pitch to Gilliam was a called strike. Old Gus had started out in front. Gilliam slapped a one-two pitch to Aparicio, who made the put-out throw to Kluszewski, and Chicagoans unleashed a roar that had been pent up for forty years.

After Wally Moon's pop-up, Charlie Neal punched out a single off Goodman's glove, then stole second with Duke Snider at bat. Snider finally drew a walk. Wynn gritted and went to work on Norm Larker, the Dodger right fielder who once had been a White Sox. Larker's liner to Rivera pulled Wynn out of the jam, and home-town fans settled back to see

Ted Kluszewski smashed his way into the hearts of Sox fans with his World Series slugging.

what their dandies would do against the National League's best.

Craig curved in a called strike, and on the next pitch Aparicio popped up. King-sized cheers greeted the first appearance of Nellie Fox. The Mighty Mite waited out Craig and walked. He scooted to third on Jim Landis's single over second, and now the Go-Go Sox were going.

Big Klu's single past Hodges did all sorts of things; it scored Nellie Fox with the first White Sox World Series run in forty years; it sent Landis to third; and it sent Chuck Churn, a right-hander, into the Dodger bull pen. Lollar drove deep to Larker at the fence, some 400 feet away. Landis tagged up after the catch and loped in to score. Billy Goodman lined out to Snider, but the White Sox were two runs in front!

Wynn set down the Dodgers' Hodges, John Roseboro, and Maury Wills, in the Los Angeles second. Chicago's Smith, Rivera, and Wynn also went out in order. The Dodgers went down again 1-2-3 in the third, Neal grounding out to retire the side after poking a foul ball "homer" into the left field stands.

Then the bottom fell out for Los Angeles, and Chicago went hysterical.

The big third started uneventfully, with Little Looey lining to Larker. But then Fox smacked a double into the right field corner, and Landis shot a single over Neal's head, bringing in Nellie and sending pitcher Clem Labine into the Dodger bull pen to warm up alongside Churn. Kluszewski routed Craig with a high fly that floated in a cross wind and fell beyond the reach of Larker into the right field stands.

With the Sox lead 5–0, in came Churn for more trouble. Lollar's fly into left center looked like an easy out, but Duke Snider and Wally Moon collided and let the ball fall for a two-base error! Goodman singled past Hodges, and Lollar scored. Smith doubled off the left center wall, and Snider made a wild throw, permitting Goodman to cross the plate.

By now the Chicago fans were as wild as the Dodger fielders.

Smith, who had taken third on Snider's wild throw, sailed for home as Rivera bounded to Neal. Trying to nip Smith at the plate Neal threw into the dirt, and another Chicago run — the sixth of the inning — went onto the Chesterfield scoreboard. Rivera pulled up at second, then streaked in on Wynn's double to left center.

Now Aparicio, who had made the only Chicago out of the inning, came up again and made the second. And finally Wills threw out Fox at first to end the debacle. Chicago had added seven runs on six hits and three Dodger errors. 9–0!

Moon beat out a bunt and Hodges singled in the Dodger fourth, but Roseboro struck out to end the threat.

Landis opened the White Sox fourth with his third successive hit of the game. Kluszewski followed with his third successive hit, and second consecutive homer. This time there was no doubt about Big Klu's clout. The ball bounded into the upper right field deck, barely inside the foul line, and about 400 feet from the plate.

Labine, the ancient reliever, took over from Churn. Clem was more of a problem, and the White Sox were unable to add to their 11–0 lead.

Wynn had it easy in the Dodger fifth.

The start of Chicago's fifth inning found a lefty, Sandy Koufax, hurling for the Dodgers. Perhaps Los Angeles should have started him, because the White Sox went hitless in the two innings Sandy toiled.

Neal got a single off Wynn in the sixth. Wills singled in the seventh, but Ron Fairly, batting for Koufax, bounded out. Sandy's successor, right-hander Johnny Klippstein, was troubled in the Chicago seventh only by Smith's double.

Wynn had been rolling along like Ol' Man River, but Gilliam led off the eighth with a single to left. When Wynn's next two pitches were balls, Manager Lopez came out to confer. With an 11–0 lead and Early complaining of stiffness in his right elbow, Lopez saw no sense of risking his ace. He called in Gerry Staley.

Staley got Neal to ground into a double play, then threw out Moon at first. In the Dodger ninth, Larker and Hodges hit back-to-back singles, but Carl Furillo flied to Smith to seal the first White Sox World Series victory since October 8, 1919.

In the Dodger dressing room, Manager Alston moaned, "We had the Chicago speed figured out, but nobody told us about all this power."

Meanwhile the jubilant White Sox were saluting their man of the hour. Big Klu, considered by many a has-been, had rewritten the book. Besieged by writers, cameramen, and well-wishers, Kluszewski talked happily of the game and his career: "Two home runs! This is the greatest thrill I've ever had in baseball, greater than those three homers in that double-header against Pittsburgh. It's absolutely the biggest moment of my career.

"I didn't think the first one was going out. Craig pitched me a slider, tight. I've got good power inside and swung at it, but at first I thought I'd missed a clean hit, and cussed myself. I really ran on that one, and at third I waved to my wife, Eleanor. They tell me she nearly fell from her seat when the ball dropped in. She missed it with her movie camera, but she got the second one. Man, is that going to be a pretty picture.

"I've got power outside, too, and when Churn sort of hung that curve, I swung. I knew that second one was going out and I hot-dogged it around the bases. Thought I'd give 'em a little of the Cadillac treatment. I knew that second one was a homer.

"That stop I made on Roseboro's grounder in the ninth? I'm glad you asked; now I can tell you that I'm a heckuva good glove man.

"No, I haven't suddenly gotten back my power. Never lost it. But with the Pirates, I wasn't playing — they were going along with Dick Stuart — and my timing was off. When I came to the White Sox and started playing, the timing began to come back.

"I've lost more than five pounds since the Sox got me in August. I weigh 242 to 245 now. Was up past 250. When I was end on the '45 Indiana team that won the Big Ten championship I weighed about 210. Didn't start growing until I left college.

"I was thirty-five on September 10. This is a late birthday present, and a great one. I figured that I'd wind up my baseball career without ever having been in a World Series."

Now the bat boy, who had been scraping mud off Klu's cleats, said, "These shoes ought to go into the Hall of Fame!"

"And have Klu play the rest of the Series barefoot?" snarled Sharkey.

Kluszewski laughed, said his wife was waiting for him, and went in for his shower.

The White Sox had a one-game lead; Chicago hearts were light. The Dodgers were uncertain, and had named Johnny Podres, the lefty pitching star of their '55 conquest of the Yankees, to go against Chicago's sensational sophomore, Bob Shaw. Manager Lopez was firm in his decision to stick with Shaw despite the grandstand managers' opinion he should use lefty Billy Pierce before the Series moved to the grotesque Coliseum.

October 2, 1959. The White Sox were now 9–5 favorites to turn back the Dodgers in the Series. Mrs. Roni Wear, a twenty-nine-year-old lady steeplejack, had scaled the center field flagpole and repaired the snarled pulley. Senator John Kennedy (D., Mass.) sat in Mayor Daley's box.

By the time Shaw began his warm-up, Comiskey Park was packed with 47,368 paying customers. Concessionaires were doing a land-office business. Vending manager Nicholas Diaz hoped for another Dodger rout, explaining, "When the game gets dull, the patrons get hungry and thirsty and we get happy about the results." Nicholas J. LaPapa, president of Vendors

Local 236, reported, "The lowest-scale man earned $75 on commissions alone for Thursday, and took in at least another $15 in tips."

Came the first pitch, and the girls sighed as handsome Bob Shaw threw out Junior Gilliam. Charlie Neal lined to Jim McAnany, the youthful White Sox outfielder who had made the jump from Colorado Springs to the World Series in one year. Consecutive singles by Wally Moon and Duke Snider were wasted as Larker flied out to McAnany.

Chicago came up. Little Looey lined a double inside first base, went to third on Nellie Fox's deep fly to Larker. Jim Landis walked and young Larry Sherry began throwing in the Los Angeles bull pen. Podres bore down, got Kluszewski to hit a double-play grounder. But Neal bobbled the ball, and while he recovered in time to throw out Kluszewski, Aparicio scored. Then Landis came in on Lollar's slow single past Neal. Chicago left the first inning with a 2–0 lead.

Maury Wills and Podres hit singles in the Dodger second, and John Roseboro was credited with a single in the fourth when Aparicio, tottering off balance, dropped a twisting looper. In the Los Angeles fifth, Shaw's spell was broken. Neal smacked his first pitch into the lower left field stands, some 350 feet out, and the score was Chicago, 2; Los Angeles, 1.

So it remained until the seventh when, with two away, Dodger manager Alston sent up big Chuck Essegian, the former Stanford football player, to pinch-hit for Podres. With the count three balls and one strike, Essegian took a tremendous cut. The ball rocketed into the upper deck of left center field. It was 2–2.

Essegian's homer, the seventh pinch-hit circuit smash in World Series history, was only the beginning of young Shaw's troubles. Junior Gilliam walked on a 3 and 1 pitch; and with one strike on him, Charlie Neal stroked a long drive to Billy Pierce in the Chicago bull pen. The Chesterfield scoreboard read 4–2 in favor of Los Angeles, and Turk Lown, a black jacket draped over his right arm, ambled in to replace Shaw.

The play that might have decided the World Series. Lollar is nailed at the plate, killing the second-game rally.

Lown walked Moon, but Snider ended the rally with a fly to Jim McAnany.

Larry Sherry, smiling Dodger right-hander who had been a California high school teammate of Chicago pitcher Barry Latman, now made his first World Series appearance. The White Sox were about to meet their master.

Sherry's slants sent down Aparicio, Fox, and Landis, in the Chicago seventh. But in the eighth, an inning to be long remembered and frequently replayed, Kluszewski led off with a single to center, went to second as Sherman Lollar singled off Gilliam's left shoulder. With none out, the White Sox had two of baseball's slowest men on base.

Earl Torgeson was sent in to run for Kluszewski. Many second-guessers felt there should also have been a runner for Lollar. Al Smith went up with orders to sacrifice the runners on. Smith fouled one, took a strike, and looked at three consecutive balls. Torgeson and Lollar were off on Sherry's next pitch, which Smith drove to the left center field wall.

Torgeson scored easily. Coach Cuccinello was giving the full-speed-ahead signal, but Lollar lost sight of the drive and tarried near second. When Lollar finally charged on, it was too late. Moon snared the loose ball, rifled a perfect throw that Maury Wills relayed unerringly to catcher Roseboro. The thousands of White Sox fans could see that Lollar was going to be out by the proverbial mile. He didn't even try to slide.

Lollar's out broke the back of the Chicago rally. With Smith waiting on third base, Billy Goodman struck out for Bubba Phillips, and Jim Rivera fouled out for Jim McAnany.

In the Dodger ninth Gilliam singled but died on second. Then Norm Cash, Lu Aparicio, and Nellie Fox were snuffed out by Sherry. The Dodgers had won, 4–3; the World Series was all tied up, one game to one; and the Windy City went into a state of shock.

In the Dodgers' dressing room after the game, Charles Leonard Neal, all 156 pounds of him, and hefty Chuck Essegian were the photographers' main targets. Relief pitcher Larry Sherry received little attention. His big days were still to come!

Coach Tony Cuccinello was on the griddle in the White Sox dressing room. He explained, "I sent Lollar in all the way. He was running on the three-two pitch. I figure the way the ball's hit he's got to score. I was watching the ball, not Lollar, and didn't know that he slowed up at second. So I kept waving him on, yelling 'Go! Go!' I know if they throw to third he's got to score and if they throw to the plate, Smith will be at third with the winning run.

"When he finally went by me, though, I could tell. If I'd

figured the relay was going to be done that way, I wouldn't have sent him in."

Lollar said, "I thought there was a chance Smith's hit might be caught, so I stopped dead at second. If he does catch it, I have no chance to get back to first."

Manager Lopez, tired but co-operative, said, "I can't criticize Cooch. It was the right play. It just didn't work."

With night closing in, some of the reporters hurried on to Midway. Others lagged behind, waiting for jets from O'Hare. Then came White Sox wives nursing virus infections, Dodger wives beefing about their poor seats in Comiskey Park. Everyone was heading for the big money in Los Angeles.

Los Angeles, October 3, 1959. Crowds milled about in the lobby of the Biltmore Hotel, pressing the White Sox for autographs. I found Manager Al Lopez in a corner and asked him, "What about Billy Pierce?"

Al said, "If Pierce had been pitching well lately, I'd have started him in the second game instead of Shaw. But he was racked pretty well at the end of the season. On the other hand, Dick Donovan looked pretty good in Detroit, and I'd rather have a right-hander going in the Coliseum."

With that Lopez and the players boarded the bus to go out to their workout. They joked en route, but on entering the Coliseum they stopped and shook their heads at the 42-foot screen that stretched from the left field foul line to a left center field mark 142 feet out. Dick Donovan said, "In this silly stadium, I'd bunch my three outfielders to the right and let Lu Aparicio play left field. Does anyone ever make an out here?"

Lopez said, "The screen doesn't hit you in the eye like the high green fence in Fenway Park. That's because you can see the seats here."

Al Smith added, "It's going to be rough hitting against a background of white shirts. The mound looks mighty close. I'll bet Drysdale looks like he's stepping in your face."

The Sox went through two hours of batting practice. Surprisingly, young Jim McAnany was the only one to loft a ball over the Chinese screen.

On the ride back to the Biltmore, Lopez told his athletes, "You have to stay natural. Can't let the screen get you. A batter would be foolish to change his style because of it."

The White Sox were wary of the Coliseum, but they were confident. For the evening ahead, some had movie plans. A few had tickets for Nancy Kelly in *A Mighty Man Is He*. Traveling secretary Bernie Snyderworth had gotten reservations for Dick and Patricia Donovan at Bob Cobb's Hollywood Brown Derby. Joe Meegan had lined up Mr. and Mrs. Billy Pierce and Mr. and Mrs. Nellie Fox for the early show at the Cocoanut Grove. Everyone was relaxed; no one was going to choke up.

Sunday morning several of the players went to church. Donovan remarked to Veeck, "Well, they can't say I don't have a prayer."

The first of a record crowd of 92,294 just was beginning to trickle into the Coliseum when the White Sox checked in. This crowd paid a record $549,071.76 — $225,000 more than the two-game receipts in Chicago. The audience surpassed the previous mark of 86,386 sitting in on the fifth game of the 1948 Series in Cleveland.

Zach Wheat, former Dodger great and a member of the Hall of Fame, delivered the opening pitch. Then Lu Aparicio made the first World Series out in Los Angeles history, going down on a 3-2 strike delivered by six-foot, five-inch Don Drysdale. A single by Landis was Chicago's only threat in the first inning. Donovan singled in the second, Lollar and Goodman hit a pair in the third, and Aparicio got a single in the fourth. Fox and Goodman hit in the fifth. By the time six innings had been completed, the White Sox had put eleven runners on base, and hadn't been able to bring one home. Dodger catcher John Roseboro had thrown out three of the Go-Go gang — Aparicio, Rivera, and Fox — on attempted steals of second. Fortunately Donovan had held the Dodgers

Aparicio meets up with another speedster, the Dodgers' Charlie Neal, who slides safely into second in a Series game.

to one hit — a fluke single by Gil Hodges, that Al Smith lost against the background of white shirts.

In the seventh, after two more wasted Sox singles by Aparicio and Fox, the dam broke. With one down, Neal singled off the screen, then scampered to second as Fox threw out Wally Moon. Donovan pitched cautiously to Norm Larker — too cautiously. Four successive pitches were balls.

Now, with those Los Angeles trumpets blaring in the stands, a walk to Hodges filled the bases. Lopez called in Gerry Staley. Dodger manager Alston's reply was to send up Carl Furillo to bat for Don Demeter. Furillo took Staley's first sinker for a strike. The second pitch he hit up the middle. Aparicio made a rush for it, but the ball went by him, and Neal and Larker scored.

That 2–0 Los Angeles lead provided the margin. Young Larry Sherry slammed the door when Drysdale faltered in the eighth-inning Chicago uprising. The final score: 3–1. The Sox were behind in games, two to one.

As soon as it was over, the second-guessing began. Bare-chested and sitting on an equipment trunk in the White Sox dressing room, Aparicio said, "The ball jumped over my glove at the last second. There was no chance. I always get that kind easy, but not this one. Yes, I got a good start on the ball. I never start better, ever.'"

In the confusion, a few believed they heard Aparicio say that the white shirts behind the plate had made it difficult for him to follow the ball as it left Furillo's bat. Lopez said, "Lu should've stretched for the ball with his gloved hand, instead of using both. He'd have had a much better chance to adjust and at least knock down the ball."

There was a rush of writers to interview almost everyone in California on the play. Former White Sox managers Paul Richards and Lew Fonseca thought that Aparicio had been slow reacting. But Walter Alston said, "The ball took a bad hop, or Aparicio would have had it."

The controversy still was going on next morning, Monday,

so at the Coliseum I buttonholed Aparicio and said, "Forget all the other opinions. Did you or did you not say that you got a good jump on that ball?"

"I told you I never got a better jump on a ball in my life," said Little Looey. "I catch it easy if it don't hop over my glove."

Early Wynn, whose right elbow had stiffened in the opener, was handed the assignment of pitching Chicago back into a tie. Roger Craig was given the Dodger call. Chicago failed with three runners on in the first, and with two runners on in the third. The Dodgers caught up with Wynn in their third, scoring four times after two batters had been retired.

Consecutive singles by Wally Moon and Norm Larker ignited the Dodger outburst. Contributing to the White Sox troubles were errors by Landis and Aparicio, a passed ball, and Gil Hodges' fly ball that fell for a single. Moon, Larker, Hodges, and Don Demeter collected the Los Angeles runs before Turk Lown came in to get Wills to ground to Fox.

Billy Pierce finally got the summons. He took over for Lown in the fourth and checked the Dodgers in the fourth, fifth, and sixth, then yielded to pinch hitter Earl Torgeson starting the Chicago seventh. Torgeson was thrown out by Neal.

Landis got a single and went to second as Aparicio attempted and failed to beat out a bunt. Then Fox dribbled a hit by Craig, Big Klu singled in Landis, and it was 4–1. Alston went to the mound to confer with Craig and decided to go on with his pitcher. Sherman Lollar proved the error of that judgment by dropping a home run over the left field screen.

Suddenly it was 4–4!

But not for long. Gil Hodges broke the deadlock with an eighth-inning homer off Staley, and that made the final score 5–4. The Dodgers had a three-to-one-game lead in the Series, and the crowd of 92,500, another new record attendance, trekked to the exits confident that their heroes would end it on the morrow. Our White Sox trudged to the dressing room determined to fight back, but from Manager Lopez to traveling secretary Bernie Snyderworth they realized chances were against them getting this World Series back to Chicago.

Nor would the Series have returned to Comiskey Park had it not been for Dick Donovan. Before 92,706, a third consecutive World Series attendance mark, Dick's lionhearted clutch pitching was backed up by Nellie Fox, who crossed the plate for the only run in the 1–0 thriller; Jungle Jim Rivera, who made a game-saving circus catch; and trainer Ed Froelich who, suddenly inspired, discarded the white stockings specially ordered for the Series and outfitted the White Sox in their regular black and red socks.

Going into the seventh inning, Chicago's Bob Shaw was bearing down on every pitch to preserve the one run that scored on Lollar's double-play ball in the fourth. With Dodgers on second and third and Charley Neal taking dead aim at the screen, Al Lopez moved Al Smith to left field to replace Jim McAnany, and sent Rivera to Smith's post in right. The switch worked like a charm though, as Lopez later confessed, it was designed to put Smith's defensive strength in left, rather than Rivera's in right.

Rivera, meanwhile, was doing some heavy thinking out there in right. Knowing Neal from experience in the Puerto Rican league, he dropped deep and waited. Sure enough, Neal's blast went to right center rather than to left. Rivera took off at the crack of the bat, spied the ball against the background, and made a dazzling, over-the-shoulder catch.

Shaw was out of trouble and, back in Chicago, Harry Creighton and Les Price and Emil Campana and all the other Go-Go White Sox fans said, My, wasn't that Al Lopez a smart manager to have sent in Rivera.

The respite for Chicago fans was a temporary one, because the Dodgers were back knocking in the eighth in one of the most nerve-racking innings in all World Series history. Moon led off with a fly to center. Landis had trouble spotting the ball and finally crouched to make the catch. The ball hit part

"That's all, Early," says Lopez as Lollar consoles Wynn in the Series' final game.

of his glove and bounded off for a single. Larker drove a 3-2 pitch deep to right and again Rivera made a saving catch. Nemesis Hodges was next up and lashed a mighty blow to left — foul by a few feet. The crowd sighed.

Lopez sauntered out for a conference, left Shaw in to finish pitching to Hodges. The great Dodger powered a low liner by Nellie Fox. Landis scooped up the ball and fired to third. Moon's slide beat the ball, with Hodges churning on to second. Shaw had had it.

Lopez called in Billy Pierce to pitch to Ron Fairly, a left-handed hitter who had been rushed up to bat for Don Demeter. Pierce's arrival inspired Alston to replace Fairly with Rip Repulski, a right-handed hitter. But first base was open, so Lopez ordered Pierce to issue an intentional walk to Repulski.

With Moon on third, Hodges at second, and Repulski on first, lefty John Roseboro was scheduled to face Pierce's slants. Instead, Alston sent up Carl Furillo, the right-handed hitter who had sabotaged the White Sox in the opener in the Coliseum.

Lopez yanked Pierce and brought in Dick Donovan. Then on the way to the dugout he paused to caution third baseman Bubba Phillips about a squeeze.

Donovan's first pitch to Furillo was a ball. Then, strike one, called. A high foul sent Lollar scrambling to the screen, the ball falling from his finger tips. Calmly, Donovan threw a low fast ball, and Furillo popped to Phillips. Two away.

It was up to Don Zimmer, now. Zimmer took a strike, then sent a lazy fly to Al Smith. The White Sox were out of the eighth.

Downtown, in the Biltmore Hotel, pretty Pat Donovan — a bride of a month — paused in her prayers to St. Jude and began hugging and kissing Mrs. Jim (Kitty) Rivera. For Dick Donovan, though, there still was the Dodger ninth.

White Sox leading, 1–0, and the Dodgers up for their last chance. Lopez's final admonition to Donovan: "Get it over, and keep it low." Larry Sherry, the pitching whiz, came up to pester Chicago in a pinch hitter's role. In the corridor outside the dressing rooms, Shaw sat with eyes fixed on a television set, muttering, "Go hard, Dick. Go hard!"

Sherry was thrown out by Phillips. Nellie Fox threw out Junior Gilliam. One out from victory. Donovan wiped perspiration from his brow and took Lollar's signal. To the television set, Shaw pleaded, "Now you've got to go hard, Dick. Go hard!" Donovan went hard on Charlie Neal, and suddenly it was over. The White Sox had won, 1–0, and the Series was going back to Chicago. It was going back with the Dodgers' lead cut to three games to two.

The White Sox ran whooping up the ramp to the shower. Passing the knot of writers and photographers, Early Wynn called, "Well, we're heading back to the baseball park." Other White Sox shouted uncomplimentary remarks about the Coliseum, and Lopez called in the writers.

"How did you feel?" they asked Tricky Dick.

Donovan's Irish eyes were smiling as he said, "How would you feel out there? I wasn't whistling 'Yankee Doodle.' "

In the Dodger room the players were quiet but television cameramen downright gloomy. Anticipating a Dodger victory they had set up to record the celebration. The sizzle of the showers was the loudest noise as they wearily folded up and stole away.

Buses sped both teams to the airport for the return to Chicago. A Los Angeles fan shook his head and asked Alston, "Is this trip necessary?"

In the air zooming east, Al Lopez kept repeating, "I said if we won this one we'd win the Series. That's still the way I feel." Early Wynn, to whom the sixth-game burden had been assigned, echoed, "It's back to the big barn, now."

More than 1,000 were at Midway airport when the White Sox charter landed at 3:18 A.M. Chants of "Go! Go! Go!" rang in the ears of the home-town players as they headed home to bed.

October 7 went down as the day that Lopez said Billy Pierce or Dick Donovan would pitch the finals after the Sox had deadlocked the Series in the sixth game. And who could say he'd be wrong?

October 8. On hand were an official 47,652, and an unofficial 600 with counterfeited tickets. It was a scoreless duel through two innings. The third brought the stroke of midnight for the Cinderella White Sox: Duke Snider homered with Wally Moon on base. The fourth opened with the Dodgers intent on boosting their 2–0 lead. They did.

Norm Larker greeted Wynn with a lead-off single. John Roseboro sacrificed, and Demeter, running for Larker, scored on Maury Wills' single to center. Starting pitcher Johnny Podres, who eventually yielded to pesty Larry Sherry, rapped a double to the center field fence, and Wills sprinted in all the way from first.

Lopez strode out, took the ball from old Wynn. Early bit his lip, slammed his fist into his glove, and trudged off. Lopez fidgeted at the mound, his eyes downcast. Donovan accepted the ball and Lopez's whispered words. But it was all over, and Lopez seemed to know it.

It didn't matter that Ted Kluszewski hit a three-run homer in the Chicago fourth, because the Dodgers stayed on the warpath. They routed Donovan. Turk Lown mopped up the fourth after Wynn and Donovan had yielded six runs in the frame.

The final score was 9–3. The Go-Go White Sox had surrendered the World Series, four games to two. All that remained for the Chicagoans was to pick up the losers' checks — a full share amounted to $7,275.17 — and wait for next year.

But Bill Veeck was not waiting for next year. As the curtain fell on the first White Sox World Series since 1919, he already was planning for '60.

Veeck and Frantic Frankie Lane of Cleveland had little trouble in making a three-for-three swap. After the smoke had cleared and the flow of mail to sports editors and club

Minnie Minoso, back where his heart belongs.

Gene Freese, strong bat acquired from Phillies.

officials subsided, the consensus was that the White Sox had come out ahead. Gone to the Indians were Bubba Phillips, John Romano, and Norman Cash. Back to the Sox came Minnie Minoso, and along with him Jake Striker and Dick Brown. Striker, a lefty pitcher, boasted a fine minor league record, and Lopez felt he had a good chance to gain a permanent spot with the club. Brown, slated for second-string catching assignments till Sherm Lollar runs out of gas, usually hits well against the Yankees.

Veeck also swung a deal with the Phillies, giving up Johnny Callison to get, as a replacement for Bubba Phillips, hard-hitting Gene Freese, who belted twenty-three home runs and drove in seventy runs in the '59 season.

With these new men, the Sox look stronger, feel stronger, and plan to do better for themselves and the South Side faithful.

Appendix

APPENDIX

WORLD SERIES

1906 (vs. Chicago Cubs)

Result: Chicago AL won 4; Chicago NL, 2.

1st Game at West Side Park, Chi., Oct. 9				R.	H.	E.
Chicago (AL)	000	011	000	2	4	1
Chicago (NL)	000	001	000	1	4	2

   Pitchers — Altrock vs. Brown.
   Attendance — 12,693

2nd Game at Comiskey Park, Chi., Oct. 10						
Chicago (NL)	031	001	020	7	10	2
Chicago (AL)	000	010	000	1	1	2

   Pitchers — Reulbach vs. White, Owen.
   Attendance — 12,595

3rd Game at West Side Park, Chi., Oct. 11						
Chicago (AL)	000	003	000	3	4	1
Chicago (NL)	000	000	000	0	2	2

   Pitchers — Walsh vs. Pfeister.
   Attendance — 13,750

4th Game at Comiskey Park, Chi., Oct. 12						
Chicago (NL)	000	000	100	1	7	1
Chicago (AL)	000	000	000	0	2	1

   Pitchers — Brown vs. Altrock.
   Attendance — 18,385

5th Game at West Side Park, Chi., Oct. 13						
Chicago (AL)	102	401	000	8	12	6
Chicago (NL)	300	102	000	6	6	0

   Pitchers — *Walsh*, White (7) vs. Reulbach, *Pfeister* (3), Overall (4).
   Attendance — 23,257

6th Game at Comiskey Park, Chi. Oct. 14						
Chicago (NL)	100	010	001	3	7	0
Chicago (AL)	340	000	01x	8	14	3

   Pitchers — *Brown*, Overall (2) vs. White.
   Attendance — 19,249

White Sox Players: G. H. White, Frank Owen, E. Walsh, N. Altrock, Roy Patterson, Frank E. Smith, Louis Fiene, pitchers; W. Sullivan, Edward W. McFarland, J. H. Hart, Jay K. Towne, catchers; J. Donohue, F. Isbell, George Rohe, Lee Tannehill, G. Davis, W. J. O'Neil, August Dundon, infielders; P. Dougherty, F. Jones, E. Hahn, outfielders. Manager: Fielder Jones.

WORLD SERIES

1917 (vs. New York Giants)

Result: Chicago AL won 4; New York NL, 2.

1st Game at Chicago, Oct. 6

				R.	H.	E.
New York (NL)	000	010	000	1	7	1
Chicago (AL)	001	100	00x	2	7	1

Pitchers — Sallee vs. Cicotte.
Homer — Felsch (Chi.)
Attendance — 32,000

2nd Game at Chicago, Oct. 7

New York (NL)	020	000	000	2	8	1
Chicago (AL)	020	500	00x	7	14	1

Pitchers — Schupp, *Anderson* (2), Perritt (4), Tesreau (8) vs. Faber.
Attendance — 32,000

3rd Game at New York, Oct. 10

Chicago (AL)	000	000	000	0	5	3
New York (NL)	000	200	00x	2	8	2

Pitchers — Cicotte vs. Benton
Attendance — 33,616

4th Game at New York, Oct. 11

Chicago (AL)	000	000	000	0	7	0
New York (NL)	000	110	12x	5	10	1

Pitchers — *Faber*, Danforth (8) vs. Schupp.
Homers — Kauff (N.Y.) 2.
Attendance — 27,746

5th Game at Chicago, Oct. 13

New York (NL)	200	200	100	5	12	3
Chicago (AL)	001	001	33x	8	14	6

Pitchers — *Sallee*, Perritt (8) vs. Russell, Cicotte (1), Williams (7),
Faber (8).
Attendance — 27,323.

6th Game at New York, Oct. 15

Chicago (AL)	000	300	001	4	7	1
New York (NL)	000	020	000	2	6	3

Pitchers — Faber vs. *Benton*, Perritt (6).
Attendance — 33,969

White Sox Players: E. V. Cicotte, U. C. Faber, E. A. Russell, C. Williams, D. C. Danforth, Joseph D. Benz, James Scott, M. G. Wolfgang, pitchers; R. W. Schalk, B. Lynn, Joseph Jenkins, catchers; C. A. Gandil, E. T. Collins, F. McMullin, G. D. Weaver, C. A. Risberg, Robert M. Byrne, R. L. Hasbrook, T. C. Jourdan, infielders; J. Jackson, O. Felsch, J. F. Collins, H. Leibold, J. Edward Murphy, outfielders. Manager: Clarence H. Rowland.

WORLD SERIES

1919 (vs. Cincinnati Reds)

Result: Cincinnati NL won 5; Chicago AL, 3.

				R.	H.	E.
1st Game at Cincinnati, Oct. 1						
Chicago (AL)	010	000	000	1	6	1
Cincinnati (NL)	100	500	21x	9	14	1

   Pitchers – *Cicotte*, Wilkinson (4), Lowdermilk (8) vs. Ruether.
   Attendance – 30,511

				R.	H.	E.
2nd Game at Cincinnati, Oct. 2						
Chicago (AL)	000	000	200	2	10	1
Cincinnati (NL)	000	301	00x	4	4	2

   Pitchers – Williams vs. Sallee.
   Attendance – 29,690.

				R.	H.	E.
3rd Game at Chicago, Oct. 3						
Cincinnati (NL)	000	000	000	0	3	1
Chicago (AL)	020	100	00x	3	7	0

   Pitchers – *Fisher*, Luque (8) vs. Kerr.
   Attendance – 29,126.

				R.	H.	E.
4th Game at Chicago, Oct. 4						
Cincinnati (NL)	000	020	000	2	5	2
Chicago (AL)	000.	000	000	0	3	2

   Pitchers – Ring vs. Cicotte.
   Attendance – 34,363.

				R.	H.	E.
5th Game at Chicago, Oct. 6						
Cincinnati (NL)	000	004	001	5	4	0
Chicago (AL)	000	000	000	0	3	3

   Pitchers – Eller vs. *Williams*, Mayer (9).
   Attendance – 34,379.

					R.	H.	E.
6th Game at Cincinnati, Oct. 7							
Chicago (AL)	000	013	000	1	5	10	3
Cincinnati (NL)	002	200	000	0	4	11	0

   Pitchers – Kerr vs. Ruether, *Ring* (6).
   Attendance – 32,006.

				R.	H.	E.
7th Game at Cincinnati, Oct. 8						
Chicago (AL)	101	020	000	4	10	1
Cincinnati (NL)	000	001	000	1	7	4

   Pitchers – Cicotte vs. *Sallee*, Fisher (5), Luque (6).
   Attendance – 13,923.

				R.	H.	E.
8th Game at Chicago, Oct. 9						
Cincinnati (NL)	410	013	010	10	16	2
Chicago (AL)	001	000	040	5	10	1

   Pitchers – Eller vs. *Williams*, James (1), Wilkinson (6).
   Homer – Jackson (Chi.)
   Attendance – 32,930.

White Sox Players: Richard Kerr, E. V. Cicotte, Claude Williams, R. H. Wilkinson, G. C. Lowdermilk, William James, J. E. Mayer, Urban C. Faber, John J. Sullivan, pitchers; R. W. Schalk, Byrd Lynn, Joseph Jenkins, catchers; C. A. Gandil, E. T. Collins, G. D. Weaver, C. A. Risberg, Fred McMullin, H. McCelland, infielders; Joseph Jackson, Harry Leibold, J. F. Collins, Oscar Felsch, Edward Murphy, outfielders. Manager: William Gleason.

WORLD SERIES

1959 (vs. Los Angeles Dodgers)

Result: Los Angeles NL won 4; Chicago AL, 2.

1st Game at Chicago, Oct. 1

				R.	H.	E.
Los Angeles (NL)	000	000	000	0	8	3
Chicago (AL)	207	200	00x	11	11	0

Pitchers — *Craig*, Churn (3), Labine (3), Koufax (5), Klipstein (7) vs. Wynn, Staley (8).

Homers — Kluszewski (Chi.) 2.

Attendance — 48,013.

2nd Game at Chicago, Oct. 2

Los Angeles (NL)	000	010	300	4	9	1
Chicago (AL)	200	000	010	3	8	0

Pitchers — *Podres*, Sherry (7) vs. Shaw, Lown (6).

Homers — Neal (L.A.) 2, Essegian (L.A.).

Attendance — 47,368.

3rd Game at Los Angeles, Oct. 4

Chicago (AL)	000	000	010	1	12	0
Los Angeles (NL)	000	000	21x	3	5	0

Pitchers — *Donovan*, Staley (6) vs. *Drysdale*, Sherry (8).

Attendance — 92,294.

4th Game at Los Angeles, Oct. 5

Chicago (AL)	000	000	400	4	10	3
Los Angeles (NL)	004	000	01x	5	9	0

Pitchers — Wynn, Lown (3), Pierce (4), *Staley* (8) vs. Craig, *Sherry* (8).

Homers — Lollar (Chi.), Hodges (L.A.).

Attendance — 92,550.

5th Game at Los Angeles, Oct. 6

Chicago (AL)	000	100	000	1	5	0
Los Angeles (NL)	000	000	000	0	9	0

Pitchers — *Shaw*, Pierce (8), Donovan (8) vs. *Koufax*, Williams (8).

Attendance — 92,706.

6th Game at Chicago, Oct. 8

Los Angeles (NL)	002	600	001	9	13	0
Chicago (AL)	000	300	000	3	6	1

Pitchers — Podres, *Sherry* (4) vs. *Wynn*, Donovan (4), Lown (4), Staley (5), Pierce (8), Moore (9).

Homers — Snider (L.A.), Moon (L.A.), Kluszewski (Chi.), Essegian (L.A.)

Attendance — 47,653.

White Sox Players: Rudolpho Arias, Dick Donovan, Barry Latman, Omar Lown, Ken McBride, Ray Moore, Bill Pierce, Bob Shaw, Gerry Staley, Early Wynn, pitchers; Earl Battey, Sherman Lollar, John Romano, catchers; Luis Aparicio, Norm Cash, Sam Esposito, Nelson Fox, Bill Goodman, Ted Kluszewski, Bubba Phillips, Earl Torgeson, infielders; Jim Landis, Jim Rivera, Al Smith, Jim McAnany, outfielders. Manager: Al Lopez.

ALL-TIME WHITE SOX ROSTER

PITCHERS

ACOSTA, Jose ('22)
ADKINS, Grady ('28-'29)
ALOMA, Luis ('50-'53)
ALTROCK, Nick ('03-'09)
APPLETON, Pete ('40-'42)
ARIAS, Rudolpho ('59)
ASH, Kenneth ('25)
BAKER, Jesse ('11)
BARNABE, Charles ('27-'28)
BARNES, Robert ('24)
BARTHOLOMEW, Lester ('32)
BEARDEN, Gene ('53)
BELL, Ralph A. ('12)
BENDER, Charles (Chief) ('25)
BENZ, Joe ('11-'19)
BIGGS, Charles ('32)
BITHORN, Hi ('47)
BLACKBURN, Foster ('21)
BLANKENSHIP, Homer ('22-'23)
BLANKENSHIP, Ted ('22-'30)
BOWLER, Grant ('31-'32)
BOWLES, E. J. ('22)
BOYLES, Harry ('38-'39)
BRADLEY, Fred ('48-'49)
BRAXTON, Garland ('30-'31)
BROWN, Clint ('36-'40)
BROWN, Harold ('51-'52)
BROWN, Joseph Henry ('27)
BRUNER, Jack ('49-'50)
BURNS, Bill ('09-'10)
BYRNE, Gerald ('29)
BYRD, Harry ('55-'56)
BYRNE, Tommy ('53)
CADORE, Leon ('23)
CAIN, Merritt (Sugar) ('36-'38)
CAIN, Bob ('49-'51, '54)
CALDWELL, Earl ('45-'48)
CALLAHAN, Jimmy ('01-'02)
CARAWAY, Pat ('30-'32)
CARRASQUEL, Alex ('49)
CASTNER, Paul ('23)
CHAKALES, Bob ('55)
CHAMBERLAIN, William ('32)
CHELINI, Italo Vincent ('35-'37)
CHOUNEAU, Chief ('10)
CICOTTE, Eddie ('12-'20)
COLE, Bert ('27)
CONNALLY, George (Sarge) ('21-'29)
CONNELLY, William('50)

CONSUEGRA, Sandalio ('53-'56)
COREY, Edward ('18)
COURTNEY, Harry ('22)
COX, Ernest ('22)
COX, George ('28)
COX, Leslie ('26)
COX, William ('37-'38)
CRABB, James Roy ('12)
CUELLAR, Charlie ('50)
CVENGROS, Mike ('23-'25)
DAGLIA, Peter ('32)
DAHLKE, Jerome ('56)
DANFORTH, Dave ('16-'19)
DAVENPORT, Jaubert ('21-'24)
DAVIS, Frank (Dixie) ('15)
DELHI, Lee (Flame) ('12)
DERRINGTON, James ('56)
DIETRICH, William ('36-'46)
DOBBS, John ('24)
DOBERNIC, Andrew (Jesse) ('39)
DOBSON, Joseph ('51-'53)
DONOVAN, Dick ('55-'59)
DORISH, Harry ('51-'55)
DOUGHERTY, Thomas ('04)
DOUGLAS, Phil ('12)
DUFF, Cecil ('22)
DUGAN, Daniel ('28-'29)
DUNKLE, Edward (Davey) ('03)
DUPEE, Frank ('01)
DURHAM, Edward (Bull) ('33)
DURHAM, James ('02)
EARNSHAW, George ('34-'35)
EAVES, Vallis ('39-'40)
EDWARDS, James ('25-'26)
EMBREY, Charles Akin ('23)
EVANS, Russell (Red) ('36)
EVANS, William Arthur ('32)
EVANS, William Lawrence ('49)
FABER, Urban (Red) ('14-'33)
FAUTSCH, Joseph ('16)
FENNER, Horace ('21)
FIEBER, Clarence ('32)
FIENE, Louis ('06-'09)
FISCHER, Charles (Carl) ('35)
FISCHER, William ('56-'58)
FLAHERTY, Patrick ('04)
FLANIGAN, Thomas ('54)
FORD, Eugene ('38)
FOREMAN, August ('24)
FORNIELES, Miguel ('53-'56)

FRASIER, Victor ('31-'33, '39)
FREEZE, Carl (Jake) ('25)
GABLER, Frank ('38)
GALLIVAN, Philip ('32-'34)
GARLAND, Louis ('31)
GARVIN, Virgil ('02)
GASTON, Milton ('32-'34)
GEBRIAN, Peter ('47)
GETTEL, Allen ('48-'49)
GICK, George ('37-'38)
GILLENWATER, Claral ('23)
GILLESPIE, Robert ('47-'48)
GOODELL, John ('28)
GOODWIN, James ('48)
GRAY, Ted ('55)
GREGORY, Paul ('32-'33)
GRIMSLEY, Ross ('51)
GRIFFITH, Clark ('01-'02)
GRISSOM, Marvin ('52)
GROVE, Orval ('40-'49)
GROTH, Ernest ('49)
GUMPERT, Randy ('48-'51)
HADLEY, Irving (Bump) ('32)
HAEFNER, Mickey ('49-'50)
HAID, Harold ('33)
HALLETT, John ('40-'41)
HAMNER, Ralph ('46)
HANSKI, Donald ('43-'44)
HARRIST, Earl ('47-'48, '53)
HARSHMAN, Jack ('54-'57)
HAYNES, Joseph ('41-'48)
HEATH, Spencer ('20)
HENRY, Frank (Dutch) ('29-'30)
HERRING, Arthur (Red) ('39)
HEVING, Joseph ('33-'34)
HODGE, Clarence (Shovel) ('20-'22)
HOLCOMBE, Ken ('50-'52)
HOLLINGSWORTH, Albert ('46)
HOVLIK, Joseph ('11)
HOWELL, Millard ('55-'58)
HUDSON, Hal ('52-'53)
HUGHES, James ('57)
HUMPHRIES, John ('41-'45)
HUTCHINSON, Ira ('33)
JACOBS, William ('27)
JAMES, William ('19)
JASPER, Harry (Hi) ('14-'15)
JOHNSON, Connie ('53, '55-'56)
JOHNSON, Don ('54)
JOHNSON, Ellis ('12, '15)
JOHNSON, John (Swede) ('45)
JONES, Sam (Sad) ('32-'35)

JORDON, Raymond (Rip) ('12)
JUDSON, Howard ('48-'52)
KATOLL, John ('01-'02)
KERIAZAKOS, Gus ('50)
KEEGAN, Bob ('53-'58)
KENNEDY, Vernon ('34-'37)
KENNEDY, William ('52)
KERR, Richard (Dick) ('19-'21, '25)
KIEFER, Joseph ('20)
KIMSEY, Clyde ('32-'33)
KINDER, Ellis ('56-'57)
KINZY, Harry ('34)
KLAERNER, Hugo ('34)
KLEPFER, Edward ('15)
KLIEMAN, Edward ('49)
KNOTT, John ('38-'40)
KOWALIK, Fabian ('32)
KRETLOW, Lou ('50-'53)
KUZAVA, Robert ('49-'50)
LAMLINE, Fred ('12)
LANGE, Frank ('10-'13)
LaPALME, Paul ('56-'58)
LATHROP, William ('13-'14)
LATMAN, Barry ('57-'59)
LAWRENCE, Robert ('24)
LEE, Thornton ('37-'47)
LEITNER, George (Dummy) ('02)
LEOPOLD, Rudolph ('28)
LEVERETTE, Gorham (Dixie)
   ('22-'24, '26)
LITLEFIELD, Richard ('51)
LOPAT, Eddie ('44-'47)
LOWDERMILK, Grover Cleveland
   ('19-'20)
LOWN, Omar ('58-'59)
LYONS, Ted ('23-'42, '46)
MACK, Frank ('22-'23, '25)
MAHONEY, Robert ('51)
MALTZBERGER, Jordon ('43-'47)
MANGRUM, Leo ('24-'25)
MANUEL, Moxie ('08)
MARCUM, John ('39)
MARLOWE, Richard ('56-'58)
MARTIN, Morrie ('54-'56)
MAYER, James Erskine ('19)
McALEESE, John ('01)
McBEE, Pryor ('26)
McBRIDE, Ken ('59)
McCABE, Richard ('22)
McDONALD, James ('56, '58)
McGUIRE, Thomas P. ('19)
McILWAIN, Stover ('57-'58)

McKAIN, Harold ('29-'32)
McMACKIN, Samuel ('02)
McWEENEY, Douglas ('21-'24)
MICHAELSON, August ('21)
MILLER, Frank ('13)
MILLER, Walter ('33)
MITCHELL, Albert ('18)
MOGRIDGE, George ('11-'12)
MOORE, James Stanford ('30-'32)
MOORE, Ray ('58-'59)
MORRIS, Joseph Bennett ('21)
MOULDER, Glen ('48)
MULRENNAN, Dominick ('21)
MURRAY, George ('33)
NELSON, Andrew ('08)
NOYES, Winfield ('19)
O'BRIEN, Thomas (Buck) ('13)
OLMSTEAD, Fred ('08-'11)
O'NEILL, Emmett ('46)
OWEN, Frank ('03-'09)
PAPAI, Al ('55-'58)
PAPISH, Frank ('45-'48)
PATTERSON, Roy ('01-'07)
PAYNE, George ('20)
PEARSON, Ike ('48)
PENCE, Russell ('21)
PERKOVICH, John ('50)
PERME, Leonard ('42, '46)
PETERS, Oscar (Rube) ('12)
PETERS, Gary ('59)
PHELPS, Raymond (Babe) ('35-'36)
PIATT, Wiley ('01-'02)
PIERCE, Walter (Billy) ('49-'59)
PIERETTI, Marino ('48-'49)
POLLET, Howard ('56)
POSER, John ('32)
PROCTOR, Edward ('23)
QUALTERS, Tom ('58)
QUINN, John Picus ('18)
RAGAN, Don (Pat) ('19)
RAYMOND, Claude ('59)
RIGNEY, John Dungan
   ('37-'42, '46-'47)
RIVIERE, Arthur ('25)
ROBERTSON, Charles ('19, '22-'25)
ROGOVIN, Saul ('51-'53)
ROSS, Lee (Buck) ('41-'45)
ROTBLATT, Marvin ('48, '50-'51)
RUDOLPH, Don ('57-'59)
RUFFING, Charles (Red) ('47)
RUSSELL, Ewell (Reb) ('13-'19)
RUSSELL, John ('21-'22)

SALVESON, Jack ('35)
SCARBOROUGH, Rae ('50)
SCHULTZ, Webb, ('24)
SCHUPP, Freddie ('22)
SCOTT, James (Death Valley)
   ('09-'17)
SCROGGINS, James ('13)
SHELLENBACK, Frank ('18-'19)
SHAW, Robert ('58-'59)
SHORES, William ('36)
SHOUN, Clyde ('49)
SIMA, Al ('54)
SKOPEC, John ('01)
SMITH, Arthur ('32)
SMITH, Clarence (Popboy) ('13)
SMITH, Edgar ('39-'43, '46-'47)
SMITH, Frank ('04-'10)
SMITH, Harry ('12)
SMITH, Robert ('13)
SPEER, Floyd ('43-'44)
STALEY, Gerry ('56-'59)
STANKA, Joe ('59)
STEENGRAFE, Milton ('24, '26)
STEWART, Frank ('27)
STINE, Lee ('34-'35)
STOBBS, Chuck ('52-'53)
STRATTON, Monty ('34-'38)
STRAHS, Richard ('54)
STRICKLETT, Elmer ('04)
SULLIVAN, John ('19)
SURKONT, Max ('49)
SUTOR, Harry ('09)
SWIFT, William ('43)
TAYLOR, Wiley ('12)
THOMAS, Alphonse (Tommy)
   ('26-'32)
THOMPSON, John ('21)
THURSTON, Hollis ('23-'26)
TIETJE, Leslie ('33-'36)
TOUCHSTONE, Clay ('45)
TROSKY, Hal Jr. ('58)
TRUCKS, Virgil ('53-'55)
TWOMBLY, Edwin (Cy) ('21)
UHLE, Robert ('38)
VALENTINETTI, Vito ('54)
VANCE, Joseph ('35)
WADE, Jacob ('42-'44)
WALSH, Jr., Edward ('28-'32)
WALSH, Sr., Edward ('04-'16)
WEHDE, Wilbur ('30-'31)
WEILAND, Edwin ('40-'42)
WEILAND, Robert ('28-'31)

WHITE, Guy Harris (Doc) ('03-'13)
WHITEHEAD, John ('35-'39)
WIDMAR, Al ('52)
WIENECKE, John ('21)
WIGHT, William ('48-'50)
WILKENSON, Roy ('19-'22)
WILLIAMS, Claude (Lefty) ('16-'20)
WILLIAMSON, Silas ('28)
WILSON, James ('56-'58)
WILSON, Roy ('28)
WISE, Archibald ('32)
WOLFGANG, Mel ('14-'18)
WOODWARD, Frank ('23)
WYATT, John Witlow ('33-'36)
WYNN, Early ('58-'59)
YOUNG, Irving ('10-'11)

CATCHERS

ARMBRUSTER, Charles ('07)
AUTRY, Martin (Chick) ('29-'30)
BATTEY, Earl ('55-'59)
BATTS, Matt ('54)
BERG, Moe ('26-'30)
BERRY, Charles ('32-'33)
BERRY, Claude ('04)
BISCHOFF, John ('25)
BLOCK, Jimmy ('10-'12)
BURNS, Joseph ('24)
CAITHAMER, George ('34)
CARREON, Camilo ('59)
CASTINO, Vincent ('43-'45)
COURTNEY, Clint ('55)
CROUSE, Clyde (Buck) ('23-'30)
DALY, Tom ('13-'15)
DeVORMER, Al ('18)
DICKEY, George (Skeets) ('41-'42, '46-'47)
DORMAN, Charles (Dutch) ('23)
EASTERLY, Ted ('12-'13)
ERAUTT, Joseph ('50-'51)
FEHRING, William ('34)
FERNANDEZ, Edward ('46)
GARRITY, Francis (Hank) ('31)
GRABOWSKI, John ('24-'26)
GRAHAM, Roy ('22-'23)
GRUBE, Frank ('31-'33, '35-'36)
HAIRSTON, Sam ('51)
HART, James ('05-'07)
HAYES, Frank (Blimp) ('46)
HENLINE, Walter (Butch) ('30-'31)
HEYDON, Michael ('04)

HUGHES, Edward ('02)
JACOBS, Otto ('18)
JENKINS, Joseph ('17, '19)
JOHNSON, Darrell ('52)
JONNARD, Clarence ('20)
JORDAN, Thomas ('44, '46)
KREITZ, Ralph (Red) ('11)
KUHN, Walter (Red) ('12-'14)
LAPP, Johnny ('16)
LEES, George ('21)
LINDSTROM, Charles ('58)
LOLLAR, Sherman ('52-'59)
LONG, James ('22)
LYNN, Byrd ('16-'20)
MADJESKI, Edward ('34)
MALONE, Edward ('49-'50)
MAYER, Walter ('11-'15)
McCURDY, Harry ('26-'28)
McFARLAND, Edward ('02-'07)
MASI, Philip ('50-'52)
MEYER, William ('13)
MOSS, Lester ('55-'58)
NIARHOS, Gus ('50-'51)
OWENS, Frank ('09)
PASEK, John ('34)
PAYNE, Fred ('09-'11)
RENSA, George ('37-'39)
RIDDLE, John ('30)
ROBINSON, Aaron ('48)
ROMANDO, John ('58-'59)
ROTH, Frank ('06)
RUEL, Harold (Muddy) ('34)
SALKELD, William ('50)
SAWATSKI, Carl ('54)
SCHALK, Raymond ('12-'28)
SCHLEUTER, Norman ('38-'39)
SCHRECKENOST, Osse ('08)
SEWELL, James (Luke) ('35-'38)
SHAW, Alfred ('08)
SHEA, Meryn ('34-'37)
SHEELY, Hollis (Bud) ('51-'53)
SILVESTRI, Kenneth ('39-'40)
SLATTERY, John ('03)
STEPHENSON, Joseph ('47)
SUGDEN, Joseph ('01)
SULLIVAN, William (Billy) ('01-'14)
TANKERSLEY, Leo ('25)
TATE, Henry ('30-'32)
TIPTON, Joseph ('49)
TOWNE, Jay (Babe) ('06)
TRESH, Michael ('38-'48)
TURNER, Thomas ('40-'44)

217

WEAVER, Arthur ('08)
WEIGEL, Ralph ('48)
WHEELER, Donald ('49)
WILSON, Robert ('51-'54)
WIRTS, Elwood ('24)
YANKOWSKI, George ('49)
YARYAN, Clarence ('21-'22)

INFIELDERS

ADAMS, Bobby ('55)
ALCOCK, John (Scotty) ('14)
ALTIZER, Dave ('09)
APARICIO, Luis ('56-'59)
APPLING, Luke ('30-'50)
ATZ, John (Jackie) ('07-'09)
BAKER, Floyd ('45-'51)
BAKER, Howard ('14-'15)
BATTLE, James ('27)
BAUMER, James ('49)
BEJMA, Aloysius (Ollie) ('39)
BERGER, Joseph ('13-'14)
BERGER, Louis (Boze) ('37-'38)
BERGHAMMER, Marty ('11)
BERRY, Connie ('53)
BLACK, John (Jiggy) ('24)
BLACKBURNE, Lena ('10-'12, '14-'15, '27-'29)
BLUE, Lu ('31-'32)
BOKEN, Bob ('34)
BONURA, Zeke ('34-'37)
BOONE, Ray ('58-'59)
BORTON, William (Babe) ('12-'13)
BOYD, Robert ('51, '53, '54)
BRIDEWESER, James ('55-'56)
BRAIN, David ('01)
BRETON, Jimmy ('13-'15)
BRIEF, Anthony (Bunny) ('15)
BURKE, James ('01)
BYRNE, Robert ('17)
CARRASQUEL, Chico ('50-'55)
CASH, Norm ('59)
CAVARRETTA, Phil ('54-'55)
CHAMBERLIN, Joseph ('34)
CHASE, Hal ('13-'14)
CISSELL, Chalmer (Bill) ('28-'32)
CLANCY, John (Bud) ('24-'30)
CLARK, Harry ('03)
CLARKE, Richard ('44)
COLLINS, Eddie ('15-'26)
CONNORS, Mervyn ('37-'38)
CORHAN, Roy ('11)

CUCCINELLO, Tony ('43-'45)
CULLER, Dick ('43)
DALY, Thomas (Tido) ('02-'03)
DASHIELL, Wally ('24)
DAVIS, George ('02, '04-'09)
DAVIS, Isaac ('24-'25)
DeMAESTRI, Joe ('51)
DENTE, Sam ('52-'53)
DeVIVEIROS, Bernard ('24)
DILLINGER, Robert ('51)
DOLAN, Pat ('03)
DONOHUE, John (Jiggs) ('04-'09)
DROPO, Walt ('55-'58)
DUNDON, Augustus ('04-'06)
DYKES, James ('33-'39)
ELLIOTT, Robert ('53)
ENGLISH, Charles ('32-'33)
ENS, Anton (Mutz) ('12)
ESPOSITO, Sam ('52, '55-'59)
EVERS, Johnny ('22)
FAIN, Ferris ('53-'54)
FARRELL, Kirby ('45)
FLASKAMPER, Ray ('27)
FONSECA, Lewis ('31-'33)
FOURNIER, Jack ('12-'17)
FOX, Jacob Nelson ('50-'59)
FRENCH, Charles ('10)
FRENCH, Raymond ('24)
GANDIL, Charles (Chick) ('10, '17-'19)
GERLACH, John ('38-'39)
GOLDSBERRY, Gordon ('49-'51)
GOODMAN, Bill ('58-'59)
GRANT, James ('42-'43)
HAAS, Bert ('51)
HANCOCK, Fred ('49)
HAPPENNY, John ('23)
HARTMAN, Fred ('01)
HASBROUCK, Robert ('16-'17)
HATFIELD, Fred ('56-'57)
HATTON, Grady ('54)
HAYES, Minter (Jackie) ('32-'40)
HICKMAN, Charles ('07)
HICKS, Buddy ('59)
HOPKINS, Marty ('34-'35)
HUNNEFIELD, William ('26-'30)
ISBELL, Frank ('01-'09)
JACKSON, Ron ('54-'59)
JEFFRIES, Irving ('30-'31)
JENKINS, John ('22)
JOHNS, William (Pete) ('15)
JOHNSON, Ernest ('12, '21-'23)

JOK, Stanley ('54, '55)
JONES, M. (Jake) ('41-'42, '46-'47)
JONES, William (Tex) ('11)
JOURDAN, Ted ('16-'18, '20)
KAMM, William ('23-'31)
KANE, John ('25)
KELL, George ('54-'56)
KENNEDY, Robert
    ('39-'42, '46-'48, '55-'57)
KERR, John ('29-'31)
KIRRENE, Joseph ('50, '54)
KLINGER, Joseph ('30)
KLUSZEWSKI, Ted ('59)
KNICKERBOCKER, William ('41)
KOLLOWAY, Donald ('40-'43, '46-'49)
KOZAR, Albert ('50)
KRESS, Charles ('49-'50)
KRESS, Ralph (Red) ('32-'34)
KRSNICH, Rocky ('49, '52-'53)
KUHEL, Joseph ('38-'43, '46-'47)
LANDENBERGER, Kenneth ('52)
LANDRUM, Jesse ('38)
LODIGIANI, Dario ('41-'42, '46)
LORD, Harry ('10-'14)
LUPIEN, Ulysses (Tony) ('48)
MAGOON, George ('03)
MANDA, Carl ('14)
MANN, John Leo ('28)
MARSH, Fred ('53-'54)
MARTIN, Joe ('59)
MAULDIN, Marshall ('34)
McCLELLAN, Harvey ('19-'24)
McCONNELL, Ambrose ('10-'11)
McMULLEN, Fred ('16-'20)
McNAIR, Donald (Boob) ('39-'40)
MAJESKI, Henry ('50-'51)
METZIG, William ('44)
MEYER, George ('38)
MICHAELS, Cass ('43-'50, '54)
MIRANDA, Guillermo ('52)
MOREHART, Raymond ('24, '26)
MORIARTY, George ('16)
MORRISSEY, Joseph ('36)
MULLEAVY, Gregory ('30, '32)
MULLEN, Charles ('10-'11)
MULLIGAN, Edward ('21-'22)
NAGEL, William ('45)
NALEWAY, Frank ('24)
NESS, Jack ('16)
ORENGO, Joseph ('45)
OSTERGAARD, Robert ('21)
OWEN, Marvin ('38-'39)

PADDOCK, Del ('12)
PARENT, Fred ('08-'11)
PECKINPAUGH, Roger ('27)
PETERSON, Carl (Buddy) ('55)
PIET, Tony ('35-'37)
PHILLIPS, Bubba ('59)
PINELLI, Ralph (Babe) ('18)
POMORSKI, John ('34)
PURTELL, William ('08-'10)
QUILLIN, Lee ('06-'07)
RADAR, Donald ('13)
RATH, Maurice ('12-'13)
REDFERN, George ('28-'29)
REILLY, Bernard ('09)
REYNOLDS, Daniel ('45)
RHAWN, Robert ('49)
RHYNE, Harold ('33)
RISBERG, Charles (Swede) ('17-'20)
ROBINSON, Eddie ('50-'52)
ROCK, Lester ('36)
RODRIGUEZ, Hector ('52)
ROHE, George ('05-'07)
RYAN, Connie ('53)
RYAN, John Collins (Blondy) ('30)
SCHALK, Roy ('44-'45)
SCOTT, Lewis (Deacon) ('26)
SELPH, Carey ('32)
SHEELY, Earl ('21-'27)
SHIRES, Arthur ('28-'30)
SHUGART, William ('01)
SIGAFOOS, Francis ('29)
SMITH, Ernest ('30)
SOUCHOCK, Steve ('49)
STEPHENS, Vernon ('53, '55)
STRANG, Samuel ('02)
SULLIVAN, William, Jr. ('31-'33)
SWANSON, Karl ('28-'29)
SWENTOR, August ('22)
TANNEHILL, Lee ('03-'12)
TERRY, Zeb ('16-'17)
THOMAS, Leo ('52)
TORGESON, Earl ('57-'59)
TORSKY, Hal ('44, '46)
VON KOLNITZ, Alfred ('16)
WALLAESA, John ('47-'48)
WARD, Aaron ('27)
WAY, Robert ('27)
WEAVER, George (Buck) ('12-'20)
WEBB, James (Skeeter) ('40-'44)
WELLS, Leo, ('42-'46)
WHITMAN, Walter ('46, '48)
WILLINGHAM, Thomas ('30)

WRIGHT, Edward ('16)
WRIGHT, Forest Glenn ('35)
YORK, Rudolph ('47)
ZEIDER, Rollie ('10-'13)

OUTFIELDERS

ABRAMS, Cal ('56)
ADAMS, Herbie ('48-'50)
ANDERSON, Harold ('32)
ANDERSON, John ('08)
ARCHDEACON, Maurice ('23-'25)
BARNES, Emile (Red) ('30)
BARRETT, William ('23-'29)
BARROWS, Roland (Cuke) ('09-'12)
BEALL, John ('13)
BEARD, Ted ('57-'58)
BERRENS, Joe ('12)
BLACKERBY, George ('28)
BOCEK, Milton ('33-'34)
BODIE, Frank (Ping) ('11-'14)
BOONE, Ike ('27)
BORDAGARAY, Stanley (Frenchy) ('34)
BOWERS, Grover ('49)
BOWSER, James (Red) ('10)
BRATCHI, Fred ('21)
BROWNE, George ('10)
BUSBY, Jim ('50-'52, '55)
CASH, Norman ('58-'59)
CALLAHAN, Jimmy ('02-'05, '11-'13)
CAMPBELL, Bruce ('30-'32)
CARNETT, Ed ('44)
CALLISON, John ('58-'59)
CHAPMAN, William (Ben) ('41)
CHAPPEL, Larry ('13-'15)
CHOUINARD, Felix ('10-'11)
CHRISTOPHER, Lloyd ('47)
CLARK, Alfred ('53)
COAN, Gil ('55)
COLE, Willie ('09-'10)
COLEMAN, Raymond ('51-'52)
COLLINS, John (Shano) ('10-'20)
CONLAN, John (Jocko) ('34-'35)
COOMBS, Cecil ('14)
CRAVATH, Clifford (Cavvy) ('09)
CURTRIGHT, Guy ('43-'46)
DELSING, James ('48-'56)
DEMMITT, Ray ('14-'15)
DICKSHOT, John ('44-'45)
DOBY, Larry ('56-'57)
DOUGHERTY, Patrick ('06-'11)

EDWARDS, Henry ('52)
EICHRODT, Fred ('31)
ELSH, Roy ('23-'25)
ENNIS, Del ('59)
FALK, Bibb ('20-'28)
FELSCH, Oscar (Happy) ('15-'20)
FOSTER, Clarence (Pop) ('01)
FOTHERGILL, Robert ('30-'32)
FRANCONA, Tito ('58)
FUNK, Elias ('32-'33)
GOODE, Wilbur ('18)
GREEN, Edward (Danny) ('02-'05)
GROTH, John ('54-'55)
GULLEY, Thomas ('26)
HAAS, George (Mule) ('33-'37)
HAFEY, Daniel (Bud) ('35)
HAHN, Ed ('06-'10)
HALLMAN, William ('03)
HARRIS, David ('30)
HARRIS, Spencer ('25-'26)
HARVEY, Edwin ('01)
HEIM, Val ('42)
HEMPHILL, Frank ('06)
HIGDON, William ('49)
HOCKETT, Oris ('45)
HOAG, Myril ('41-'44)
HODAPP, Johnny ('32)
HODGIN, Ralph ('43-'48)
HOFFMAN, Clarence ('29)
HOLMES, James (Ducky) ('03-'05)
HOOPER, Harry ('21-'25)
HUELSMAN, Frank ('04)
HOY, William (Dummy) ('01)
JACKSON, Joe ('15-'20)
JOHNSTON, Jimmy ('11)
JOLLEY, Smead ('30-'32)
JONES, Charles ('04)
JONES, David ('13)
JONES, Fielder ('01-'08)
KAVANAGH, Charles (Silk) ('14)
KELLY, Albert (Red) ('10)
KREEVICH, Mike ('35-'41)
LANDIS, Jim ('57-'59)
LANE, Dick ('49)
LEHNER, Paul ('51)
LEIBOLD, Harry (Nemo) ('15-'20)
LEIFER, Elmer ('21)
LENHARDT, Don ('51)
MALLONEE, Jules ('25)
MARSHALL, Willard ('54)
MATTICK, Walter (Chink) ('12-'13)
McANANY, James ('58-'59)

McCORMICK, Myron (Mike) ('50)
McFARLAND, Hermus ('01-'02)
McGHEE, Warren Edward ('50, '54)
McINTYRE, Matty ('11-'12)
MELE, Sam ('52-'53)
MELOAN, Paul (Mollie) ('10-'11)
MERTES, Samuel ('01-'02)
MESSENGER, Charles ('09-'11)
METKOVICH, George ('49)
METZLER, Alexander ('27-'30)
MINOSO, Orestes ('51-'57)
MOORE, Randolph ('27-'28)
MOORE, James William ('30)
MOSES, Wally ('42-'46)
MOSTIL, John ('18, '21-'29)
MUELLER, Don ('58-'59)
MUELLER, William ('42, '45)
MURPHY, Joseph (Eddie) ('15-'21)
NEIS, Bernie ('27)
NICHOLAS, Don ('52-'54)
NIEMAN, Robert ('55-'56)
NORMAN, Willis ('31-'32)
NORTHEY, Ronald ('55-'57)
O'NEILL, William (Tip) ('06)
OSTROWSKI, John ('49-'50)
PATTERSON, Hamilton ('09)
PENCE, Elmer ('22)
PHILLEY, David ('41, '46-'51, '56-'57)
PHILLIPS, John (Bubba) ('56-'59)
PLATT, Mizell (Whitey) ('46)
PORTER, Irving ('14)
POWELL, Robert ('55-'57)
PURDY, Everett ('26)
QUINLAN, Thomas ('15)
RADCLIFF, Raymond (Rip) ('34-'39)
RAPP, Earl ('49)
REYNOLDS, Carl ('27-'31)
RICKERT, Marvin ('50)
RIVERA, Manuel (Jim) ('52-'59)
ROSENBERG, Louis ('23)
ROSENTHAL, Larry ('36-'41)
ROTH, Robert ('14-'15)
ROUSH, Eddie ('13)
ROTHROCK, John ('32)
SCALA, Jerry ('48-'50)
SCHALLER, Walter ('13)
SCHREIBER, Henry ('14)
SEEDS, Robert ('32)
SEEREY, James (Pat) ('48-'49)
SHORT, David ('40-'41)
SIMMONS, Al ('33-'35)
SIMONS, Melborn ('31-'32)
SIMPSON, Harry ('59)
SKETCHLEY, Harry ('42)
SKIZAS, Lou ('59)

SMAZA, Joseph ('46)
SMITH, Al ('58-'59)
SOLTERS, Julius ('40-'43)
STEINBACHER, Henry ('37-'39)
STEWART, Eddie ('51-'54)
STONEHAM, John ('33)
STRUNK, Amos ('20-'24)
STUMPF, George ('36)
SWANSON, Evar ('32-'34)
TAITT, Douglas ('29)
TAUBY, Fred ('35)
THOMPSON, Rupert ('38-'39)
TUCKER, Thurman ('42-'47)
UHALT, Bernard ('34)
UHLIR, Charles ('34)
VELTMAN, Arthur ('26)
VINSON, Ernest ('06)
WALKER, Fred (Dixie) ('36-'37)
WALKER, Gerald (Gee) ('38-'39)
WASHINGTON, Vernon ('35-'36)
WATWOOD, John ('29-'32)
WEBB, Earl ('33)
WELDAY, Lyndon ('07, '09)
WEST, Samuel ('42)
WHITE, Eddie ('55-'58)
WILLSON, Frank ('18-'27)
WILSON, George ('52)
WILSON, Bill ('52-'53)
WOLFE, Roy ('12-'14)
WRIGHT, Tom ('52-'53)
WRIGHT, Taft ('40-'48)
ZARILLA, Al ('51-'52)
ZERNIAL, Gus ('49-'51)
ZWILLING, Edward (Dutch) ('10)

UTILITY PLAYERS

BROWN, Delos ('14)
BUBSER, Harold ('22)
CORTAZZO, John ('23)
GOLETZ, Stanley ('41)
HAJDUK, Chester ('41)
HARGROVE, William (Pat) ('18)
JACKSON, Charles ('15)
KALIN, Frank ('43)
LOVETT, Merritt ('33)
MARTIN, William ('38)
McLARRY, Paul (Polly) ('12)
MERRIMAN, Lloyd ('55)
NELSON, Glenn ('51)
PRATT, Francis ('21)
SHOOK, Raymond ('16)
SNIPES, Wyatt ('23)
F.W. TAYLOR, Leo Thomas ('23)